# Physical Characteristics of the Japanese Chin

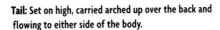

(from the American Kennel Club breed standard)

**Topline:** Level.

**Body:** Square, moderately wide in the chest with rounded ribs.

**Tail:** Set on high, carried arched up over the back and flowing to either side of the body.

**Coat:** Abundant, straight, single, and silky.

**Color:** Either black and white, red and white, or black and white with tan points.

**Hindquarters:** *Legs*—Straight as viewed from the rear and fine boned. Moderate bend of stifle. *Feet*—Point straight ahead.

# Japanese Chin

◇

By Juliette Cunliffe

# Contents

KENNEL CLUB BOOKS® **JAPANESE CHIN**
ISBN 13: 978-1-59378-329-7

Copyright © 2005 • Kennel Club Books® • A Division of BowTie, Inc.
40 Broad Street, Freehold, New Jersey 07728 USA
Cover Design Patented: US 6,435,559 B2 • Printed in South Korea

Photography by Mary Bloom and Carol Ann Johnson
with additional photographs by

Paulette Braun, T.J. Calhoun, Carolina Biological Supply,
Isabelle Français, Bill Jonas, Dr. Dennis Kunkel, Tam C. Nguyen,
Phototake, Jean Claude Revy and Alice van Kempen.

**Illustrations by Patricia Peters.**

The publisher wishes to thank all of the owners of the dogs featured in this book, including Mrs. Joy Jolley, Judy Moser, Tommy & Carla Jo Ryan, Maria Shashaty and Susan Spencer.

The engaging Japanese Chin has been prized by the fairer sex for centuries. Today the Chin delights fanciers of every persuasion all over the world.

# HISTORY OF THE

# JAPANESE CHIN

What a delightful character is the Japanese Chin, a dog that the Japanese people described as having a "butterfly head, sacred vulture-feathered feet and a chrysanthemum tail." The Chin was never allowed to run in the streets, but instead was carried in beautiful straw baskets when taken outdoors. Some ancient sources reveal that some Chin were kept in hanging baskets, much liked caged birds. That surely is sufficient to whet the reader's appetite to learn more about this charming little canine that hails from the Orient and was considered as royalty.

Dainty Japanese ladies decked their Chin out in cerise-colored ribbons, with frills around the neck. They were proud of their sweet little pets, which made them the envy of all their friends. These were fascinating little dogs, and affectionate to a degree. "Playful" was not thought sufficient a word to describe their temperament, for they never tired of playing games and were always graceful in their movements. Travelers to Japan described them as having "really attractive faces, almost human, especially the females."

In the past, the breed was known as the Japanese Pug and the Japanese Spaniel, only later acquiring the name by which it is known today. There are a number of indigenous breeds to Japan, in addition to the tiny Chin, including the diminutive Japanese Terrier, which looks rather like the Toy Fox Terrier; the Japanese Spitz, recognized in Britain, appearing much like a white German Spitz or the American Eskimo Dog; and the remarkable Shiba Inu, the smallest of the country's spitz dogs, which also include the larger Shikoku, Kishu, Kai and the giant Akita. Japan's great mastiff, once used in highly

In 1890s, small Oriental dogs, such as the Pekingese on the far left and the two Japanese Spaniels, as our breed was called for many years, were favored by nobility in the dogs' homelands and beyond.

While many of them were black and white, some were red and white or white with lemon-yellow patches.

Commodore Perry, on his famous expedition to Japan in 1857, commented that there were three articles that always formed part of an Imperial present. These were rice, dry fish and dogs. It has also been said that charcoal was also included. Four "small dogs of rare breed" were sent to the President of the United States as part of the Emperor's gift, but it was decided that two of these dogs should be put on board Admiral Stirling's ship for England's Queen Victoria.

Unfortunately, the two dogs destined for America did not survive their long journey. They were named Sam Spooner and Madame Yeddo and were put on a steam frigate heading to Mississippi, along with some Japanese cats. The dogs were described as "of the Pug character but with beautiful long

*A veritable Chinese cousin, the Pekingese has long been associated with the Chin, so much so that combined clubs for both breeds have existed.*

ritualized battles, the Tosa Inu is often classified as one of the "dangerous dogs" and is, in fact, even banned in the UK.

The Japanese Chin was known in England during the middle of the 19th century, and probably much earlier, for seamen frequently brought home such dogs for their sweethearts.

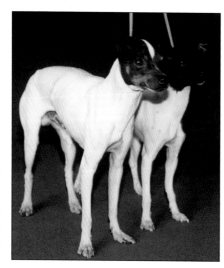

*Few people have met the Japanese Terrier in person, as it is very rare and not even commonly seen in its homeland.*

### MORE BRILLIANT THAN GOLD

Japanese Spaniels, as they were once known, were described as "not one whit behind the intelligence of the inhabitants of the island they come from." It was also said that they frequently fetched a price far in excess of their weight in gold.

**FEAST OF THE CHIN**

The recommended diet for a Japanese Chin around the turn of the 20th century included rice, which agreed particularly well with this breed, fresh fish, sheep's head, tongue, chicken livers, milk and battered pudding. Oatmeal porridge was also suitable, alternated with a little scraped raw meat as a special treat. Red meat was not considered suitable for young puppies.

attention of the Bishop of Victoria in 1861. He described them as lap dogs not more than 7 or 8 inches long and tells us that they were found in considerable numbers. Just two years later, Robert Fortune was commissioned by the Indian government to visit China and Japan to obtain information about the tea plant. Fortunately for us, he appears also to have had an interest in dogs. Mr. Fortune mentioned a dog that was bred by the Japanese people and dwarfed by the use of alcohol. He wrote of

hair, black and white in color." The two that died, along with another given to another American government official, were all buried at sea in sailor fashion, being put in shotted canvas bags.

Commodore Perry suggested that the small Japanese dogs may have been involved in the early breeding of the King Charles Spaniel in England (the breed we know as the English Toy Spaniel). He relates that in 1613 an English captain returned from a journey to Japan, carrying with him a letter from the Emperor and presents in return for those sent to him by His Majesty of England. It is indeed possible that dogs may have formed part of the gift and, if so, this Japanese breed may have been introduced to England at that time.

Ancestors of the Japanese Chin we know today attracted the

The Japanese Tosa Inu, a giant breed reaching up to 200 lb, is a formidable fighting breed that is sometimes categorized as a "dangerous dog."

A life of leisure well befits the Japanese Chin, as this portrait from the 1930s well conveys.

them as being not more than 9 or 10 inches long, with snub noses and sunken eyes, though the description of the eyes is not one that would fit the breed today. Fortune did not consider the breed in any way beautiful, but rather more curious, though he did say that the dogs were much prized by natives and foreigners alike.

Soon afterward, Sir Rutherford Alcock, who was Britain's representative at the Japanese Court, wrote of them as "little dogs, with eyes like saucers, no nose, the tongue hanging out at the side, too large for the mouth, and white and tan in color, if possible—a species of King Charles Spaniel intensified; and there is so much genuine likeness that I think it probable the Merry Monarch was indebted to his marriage with a Portuguese Princess for the original race of spaniels, as well as for the island of Bombay."

---

**RESPECT IN LIFE AND BEYOND**

Although by the 19th century, the Japanese people seemingly paid little regard to dogs, in the 18th century, every street had to maintain a given number of dogs and provide for all of their needs. Upon death, dogs were carried up to the tops of mountains and hills, where they were given very decent burials.

---

The first actual pair is believed to have arrived in Britain around 1870. Chin Chin Irst was the male, and his little mate was quaintly called Wee Woo. Although the Japanese people at that time had little interest in dogs generally, they were not anxious to sell their small dogs, so there was great difficulty in obtaining them. In Japan, such dogs around that

The Shikoku is counted among Japan's mid-size spitz breeds, along with the Ainu, Kai and Kishu.

The English Toy Spaniel shares the short muzzle and upturned nose of the Chin.

time weighed only around 2.5 lbs. Later exportations out of Japan generally weighed in the region of 7–12 pounds.

Longhaired lap dogs have been treasured by the Japanese for centuries and the Japanese, like many other Asian peoples, bred their lap dogs to such a small size that they could be conveniently carried in the sleeve or held comfortably under the chin. By 1888 Dalziel, a well-known canine author, wrote that this was a breed that had seldom been found in England, except in the homes of men who had lived in the East or who had friends there. He said that because it was difficult to rear puppies, only a few small ones could be found. In Japan, he said, the larger ones were of no value, but it was difficult to find anyone who would part with the small ones, known as "sleeve dogs."

## CONNECTIONS WITH OTHER BREEDS

Early evidence shows that Chinese Toy dogs were frequently sent to Japan, possibly as far back as 1,500 years ago when Japan began to adopt Buddhism. Chinese teachers went to Japan and it is believed that some of them took along their small dogs. In 824 AD, two pai dogs (small, short-faced, short-legged dogs) were recorded as having been sent from China as a tribute to the Emperor of Japan. The sleeve dogs, so well regarded in China, became very popular in Japan. It was said that at one time such great numbers of these dogs were taken to Japan from China that what they termed "supplies" came to an end.

We also know from Dr. Lockhart, writing in 1867, that in China there were "two kinds

### A HISTORICAL PERSPECTIVE

In 1900, Charles Henry Lane wrote of the breed, "...at the present time, I think, it enjoys the most popularity, and is kept by ladies of high rank, as well as by their humbler fellow-creatures." He also tells his readers that they had a "very quaint, old-fashioned look about them, even when puppies..." He noted that among imported specimens, the mortality rate was very high.

**PROTECTED BY THE STATE**
Kempfer's *History of Japan* tells readers that in 1727 dogs were treated with exaggerated concern. Huts were built in every street for dogs that grew old or infirm. If a dog did damage to anyone or anything, no one dared touch it, except the public executioner, and only then if given a direct order from the governors.

principal points. Firstly, the dog had to have what was called a "butterfly head," the white blaze representing the body of a butterfly and the other color, in combination with the ears, resembling the wings.

Secondly, the upper blaze of the face, that is to say the body of the butterfly, was to form the sacred "V." Thirdly, there was to be a "bump of knowledge," in the shape of a round, black or

of Pug." One of these was a small, black and white dog that was long-legged and pug-nosed, and had prominent eyes. The other, of course, is the Pug breed with which we are familiar today.

The Hon. Mrs. McLaren Morrison, who imported to Britain many foreign breeds and whose opinions commanded respect, believed that the Japanese Chin was related to the short-nosed spaniel of Tibet, now known to us as the Tibetan Spaniel. She also thought the English Toy Spaniels (King Charles Spaniels in Britain) had similar origins.

## BREED REQUIREMENTS IN JAPAN 100 YEARS AGO

In turn-of-the century Japan, particular importance was attached to markings seen in the Chin. The Japanese Chin breed standard contained five

The solid white Japanese Spitz has begun to attract admirers outside Japan, though it remains far less known than the Chin, the Akita and the Shiba Inu.

The Ainu Dog, also known as the Hokkaido Dog, represents a mid-size spitz breed of Japan. Of the Japanese spitz breeds, the Akita is the largest and the Shiba Inu is the smallest.

colored spot, on top of the head. The fourth requirement was that the Chin should be possessed of "vultures' feet," represented by their profuse feathering. Finally, the tail, when properly curled, was to display a marked similarity to the chrysan-themum, the sacred flower of Japan.

### A ROYAL FAVORITE

Before Princess Alexandra became queen, she was painted with her favorite little Japanese Chin on her lap. This portrait was exhibited, bringing great attention to the breed, which was

The Princess of Wales, later to become Queen Alexandra, is revealed here in the company of her pets, two of which were Japanese Chin.

for a while considered the "craze of the day," as indeed were many Japanese artistic works at that time. When she became queen, Alexandra still retained her affection for the breed. Visiting the Ladies' Kennel Association Show in 1903, she singled out the Japanese Chin for special notice from the parade of around 100 champions, a highly flattering tribute to the breed.

There is an amusing story of the artist Gertrude Massey painting two of Queen Alexandra's Japanese Chin. Mrs. Massey visited Buckingham Palace, where the dogs were placed in an armchair in the queen's blue and gold sitting room. The queen fluttered around, arranging the way they were to be painted, while the artist looked on. The dogs had what she described as little button noses, on one of which was a tiny lump. But the queen instructed Mrs. Massey not to include the lump in the painting. "Poor little fellow," she said, "he has had an accident. My nephew ran over him with a bicycle."

### THE JAPANESE CHIN IN THE UNITED STATES

Interest in the Japanese Chin as a show dog was apparent in America before the breed became a favorite in England. At a New York show in 1882, there were nine entries of the breed.

However, it was another, called Chico, that was considered by far the "best of the breed," but this dog had been entered in the Miscellaneous Class as a "Pekingese (China) spaniel." This dog had a wealth of coat, and his conformation was apparently of such high quality that the three judges decided to recognize the dog's merits by giving him a special prize.

As the years moved on, Japanese Chin became more of a

rarity, but early in the 20th century they were once again holding their own. Because of the steady demand for the breed by New York fanciers, there were continuous imports into Pacific Coast ports until there became a scarcity of better-quality dogs. Employees on English steamers that plied between Japan and ports on the Pacific Coast brought over such dogs to sell in bulk to local fanciers at a set price per dog. Many of these, however, were of poor quality, but there were few good ones in each lot. The early American breed standard incidentally allowed for solid-black dogs as well as the more universally recognized colors.

The Japanese Spaniel, as the breed was then called, was one of the early breeds accepted by the American Kennel Club. In 1888, the first member of the breed, named Jap, was entered in the AKC Stud Book. The first

Queen Alexandra, shortly after her ascension to the British throne, is depicted holding her devoted companion Japanese Chin.

**SLEEVE DOGS**
Probably the popular Gilbert and Sullivan operetta *The Mikado* familiarized the Western public with the capacity and cut of the Japanese sleeve. So large was it that it might comfortably have entertained a medium-sized Poodle; hence, so-called "sleeve dogs" need not necessarily have been so small as at first imagined.

ABOVE: Eng. Ch. Mr. Weejum, owned by Mrs. Stuart Rogers, won 14 Challenge Certificates during his six-year show career, having earned retirement in 1930. BELOW: Eng. Ch. Hokusai Nippon of Hove, owned by Mrs. B. A. R. Harris, was the winner of 30 first prizes during the 1930s.

champion in the breed in the USA is believed to have been Ch. Nanki Poo. A breed club was formed around this time, but later became inactive, and the Japanese Spaniel (Chin) Club of America we know today was

founded in 1912. The breed was known as the Japanese Spaniel until 1977, when its name was officially changed to Japanese Chin. Today the Japanese Chin ranks in the top half of dog breeds as per AKC registration statistics, with over 1,200 dogs registered annually.

## THE CHIN IN THE UK

Around 1890, the number of Japanese Chin entered at any show could be counted on one hand, but interest in the breed quickly increased its popularity. By 1895, there was sufficient interest in the breed for a club to be formed, breeders of Japanese Chin joining with Pekingese fanciers to form the Japanese Chin and Pekingese Club. They remained together for ten years, during which time both breeds achieved more popularity, enabling separate clubs to be established. By 1903, there were over 60 entries at England's Kennel Club shows. In terms of entries, they eclipsed many other small breeds, including the Yorkshire Terrier, the King Charles Spaniel and the Blenheim Spaniel. By 1904, it was considered that the delightful Japanese Chin had successfully and securely established itself in the dog-lover's favor, gaining a position of popularity only surpassed among "drawing-room dogs" by the ever-popular Pomeranian and Pug. The Japanese Chin Club was registered with the English Kennel Club in 1905 and grew steadily stronger until the advent of WWI.

During the war years, there was hardly any breeding, and by 1918 the breed had again become scarce. Following the war, several new kennels sprang up and the Japanese Chin Club tried hard to encourage interest in the breed, but unfortunately WWII intervened, and it was not until 1964 that England's Kennel Club annual registration figures surpassed the 100 mark. However, it was in 1946 that the first post-war Championship Show was held for the breed, this in conjunction with the Papillon, Brussels Griffon and Maltese clubs. Notably, one of the Challenge Certificates (awards needed to become an English champion) was won by Oriental Chrysanthemum, a red and white Chin bitch who went on to become the breed's first post-war champion. To add to the poignancy of this win, her sire was the last dog to gain the title of champion before war had broken out.

From then on, the breed in Britain has gone from strength to strength, although Kennel Club registrations still only range around 200, far below some of the other breeds in the

Mrs. Addis with Eng. Ch. Dai Butzu II, winner of the Rotherham Cup in 1895.

Toy Group that regularly have well in excess of four figures. But provided there is a substantial gene pool, keeping litters relatively few can be far better for a breed than having numbers soar into the thousands. The Japanese Chin is certainly here to stay, and the breed's well-being is in the capable hands of the Japanese Chin Club.

A very famous dog, Ch. Royal Yama Hito, admired for his profuse coat, was ideal for the standard in his day.

# JAPANESE CHIN

The Japanese Chin is a small, friendly and affectionate companion, one who is alert, spirited and naturally clean. Added to this, the breed is enormously good-looking, with little or no "doggy odor," provided, of course, that the coat is maintained in good condition.

It has been said that in creating the Japanese Chin, the Japanese people tried to blend both dog and cat, and there may indeed be some merit in this myth, for the breed does have fastidious cleaning habits. They often also use their front feet to "bat" and to explore, much as a cat would do. Many also have the ability to climb well and can sometimes be found in the most unlikely of places. People go so far as to say that the Japanese did not even consider the Chin to be a dog at all, but that is stretching the imagination a little too far!

Come what may, the Japanese Chin is a very special little dog, a gentle breed that gets along well with all creatures, and one that has understandably won its way into many people's hearts.

## PERSONALITY

The AKC breed standard describes the breed's temperament as "sensitive and intelligent" and "responsive and affectionate." The English breed standard refers to the breed's temperament as gay, happy and gentle, as well as good-natured, but perhaps one should add to that the words used in the standard of Japan: "Clever, mild and lovely." There are undoubtedly many more words that could be selected to describe the personality of the Chin, but "impish and delightful" spring most immediately to the author's mind.

The breed indeed uses a high degree of intelligence in relation to the big wide world that surrounds it. Although small, the Chin generally seems happy to encounter anyone or anything that he comes across. He needs, though, to be socialized, for the dog can be

## CHIN AS CHILDREN

Giving his views on the breed in 1904, Mr. George Liddell said, "Japanese Chin are the cleanest and nicest dogs I have ever known. Mine eat, drink and sleep with me, and I never find any offensive smell from them. They appear to thrive better when treated as children, and mine are very sensitive when scolded, and most affectionate—particularly the bitches."

shy or can even display fear among other dogs if not brought up to mix and mingle. Socializing a Japanese Chin, however, is not difficult to do, provided that an owner uses common sense in supervising introductions. When a Chin is allowed off-lead, an owner must also take the breed's small size into consideration, for it is sometimes easier for one of these little tots to get more confused by his surroundings than it is for larger dogs. Owners should also keep in mind that a Chin may not realize that every dog he encounters will not turn out to be his best friend!

Chin are certainly not as temperamental as many of the other Toy breeds, but are happy little characters with a down-to-earth, yet bumptious personality, making good companion dogs. Chin seem to have very individual personalities and are quite capable of showing their particular likes and dislikes.

The Japanese Chin seems destined to live inside the home, for emotional needs are high and the breed demands affection. Chin like to keep their owners in sight, and many are prone to following their owners from room to room. They are normally patient enough to wait quietly while their owners are out for a short while, but can suffer emotionally if left alone for long periods. They do enjoy their comforts around the home, and make a very endearing sight curled

**SELF-TAUGHT WONDERS**
Many Japanese Chin owners would agree that their dogs train them, rather than the other way around! Many Chin seem to have the ability to learn tricks and to teach themselves "on their own," so to speak. This often seems to come about by their careful observation of other dogs.

up in a comfortable armchair.

In terms of canine companionship, Chin seem to thoroughly enjoy being among other Chin, often in preference to other breeds. They are said to be "self aware." Having said that, they can certainly get along well with other breeds of dog, and with their alter-egos, cats, too.

## PHYSICAL CHARACTERISTICS

The Japanese Chin is an elegant and aristocratic little dog, smart in appearance and compact in balance. Its head is somewhat large in proportion to the breed's small stature, with a broad skull that is rounded both in front and between the ears. The wonderful large, dark eyes are set wide apart and the white in the inner corners of the eyes gives that characteristic look of eternal astonishment! The short, wide muzzle is well cushioned, and at the sides of the large nostrils are rounded upper lips. The well-feathered ears that frame the face so beautifully are actually V-shaped and small, but they are set high on the head and carried slightly forward.

Square in build and wide in chest, the Chin should have straight forelegs, with a good turn of stifle at the rear. Feet are rather different from those of many other breeds, being slender and shaped like the feet of a hare, so they are more elongated in shape than the more common "cat" foot found in so many dogs. Another highly attractive characteristic of this breed is the high-set tail, which is closely curved or plumed over the back in proud Japanese style.

### SIZE

In Japan, size guidelines are by height, rather than by weight. There, dogs should be about 10 inches at withers, with bitches slightly smaller. According to the AKC standard, which also specifies height but not weight, height at the withers is expected to be between 8 and 11 inches, so once more we can observe legitimate reasons for a wide variation in size, although size is much more uniform now than past decades.

To demonstrate another difference among standards of various countries, the UK standard contains no height guidelines, but does specify weight limits, requiring the Japanese Chin to fall within the weight range of 4–7 lbs. This is qualified by the statement, "Daintier the better," although type, quality and soundness should never be sacrificed to achieve daintiness. From this we can see that size can, and indeed does, vary quite considerably still within the breed. But the Chin is very much one of the Toy breeds and is perfectly at home in the Toy Group in which it is judged at dog shows.

There is no disputing the fact that this is a small breed and, therefore, more delicate in its construction than most other dogs. The Japanese Chin is better suited to a gentle kind of owner, and, although the Chin likes to play, is not suitable for rough teasing and overly boisterous games.

### COAT

I think most would agree that the long, soft, silky coat is the breed's crowning glory. It should be profuse and straight, with no curl or wave. Although straight, the coat should not lie flat to the body, but instead has a tendency to stand out, especially at the frill around the neck.

Apart from the profuse body coat, there is a substantial amount of feathering on the Japanese Chin. This is found on the ears, so that they appear considerably longer than they actually are, on the legs and on the ends of the toes. The tail, too, is profusely feathered, giving that finishing touch to this very attractive little dog.

Because the coat is long, it does require a certain amount of grooming, and this is something to bear in mind before deciding on the Japanese Chin as your chosen companion. The Chin's silky coat is perhaps surprisingly easy to keep in good condition; indeed, of the longer coated breeds, the Chin has one of the easiest coats to maintain, being a single coat.

The coat does shed seasonally, and unspayed bitches shed more than those that have been spayed, and more than males. They do not shed enormous quantities of coat in comparison with some other breeds, but they do shed, so owners should be prepared to deal with some shed hair around the home.

### Color

Black and white or red and white are two of the possible color combinations. However, the word

## HEART-HEALTHY

In this modern age of ever-improving cardio-care, no doctor or scientist can dispute the advantages of owning a dog to lower a person's risk of heart disease. Studies have proven that petting a dog, walking a dog and grooming a dog all show positive results toward lowering your blood pressure. The simple routine of exercising your dog—going outside with the dog and walking, jogging or playing catch—is heart-healthy in and of itself. If you are normally less active than your physician thinks you should be, adopting a dog may be a smart option to improve your own quality of life as well as that of another creature.

The Japanese Chin is first and foremost a companion dog who cherishes the company of loving owners.

"red" encompasses all shades of sable, lemon or orange. The brighter and clearer the red color, the better, and whatever the color, it should be evenly distributed on the cheeks and ears and as patches on the body. The white part of the coat should be clear, not flecked; that is to say, there should be no small specks of black or other color mixed in with the white areas of the coat.

The third color combination is black and white with tan points. This means that tan (or red) points appear on the following: over each eye, inside the ears, on both cheeks and at the area of the anal vent if any black appears there. It is interesting to note that the tricolor pattern is not recognized as accept-able in the UK.

### TEETH

The Chin's bite should be slightly undershot, meaning that the bottom front teeth (lower incisors) are slightly forward of the upper ones. It is important that the mouth is not wry, meaning having a slight twist or poor alignment of upper and lower jaw. This can frequently cause the tongue to hang out from the side of the mouth. The tongue should not show, so even a small tip of tongue showing at the center of the mouth is not desirable in the show ring. With old age, and subsequent loss of teeth, it is not unusual to find that a Chin's tongue does begin to show.

### HEALTH CONSIDERATIONS

The Japanese Chin, although small, is a hardy little dog, and the breed is generally a healthy one. However, as with all dogs, illness can befall the breed, so it is always wise to be aware of some of the problems that might occur.

The Japanese Chin Club of America carried out a "Health Watch Research" and a reformed health committee was put in place in March 1999, involving an increased number of people in health fields. Their aim is to concentrate on heart health in the breed, as there are heart conditions that can occur in the Chin. The JCCA's Health Committee also sponsors clinics in which exams to screen dogs for major health concerns are available.

### PATELLAR LUXATION

A problem suffered by some Japanese Chin is patellar luxation, which is trouble with the knee joints, a problem that is common to many of the Toy breeds. A symptom is when the dog limps or carries one leg off the ground when running. This is because a bone has slipped out of position, due either to injury or to poor alignment. It is an important factor that a dog so affected is not allowed to become overweight, as this is likely to exacerbate the problem.

Many dogs with patellar luxation live with the problem without experiencing pain, but surgery sometimes has to be done in more severe cases. A veterinary testing procedure is available.

### Eye Problems

Any breed with particularly large eyes is rather susceptible to sustaining damage to the eyes. It is therefore essential for eyes to be kept clear of debris and discharge. Caring for the eyes, especially with a large-eyed, long-coated breed, is an essential part of responsible dog ownership. Owners of Chin and cats should also take care that their Chin's eyes are not damaged by a cat's claws. Cat scratches can all too easily cause damage, as can rose bushes and thorny garden shrubs. Should ever there be evidence of a scratch, ulcer or heavier than usual discharge, veterinary advice should be sought without delay. Additionally, Chins can be affected by cataracts, which can be hereditary in nature but treatable.

### Heat Stroke

Occasionally, usually due to lack of suitable care in hot weather, a Japanese Chin can experience heat stroke (signs include intense panting, salivating, collapsing). Of course, this is something that can happen to any breed, but breeds with pug-like forefaces tend to be more susceptible, as breathing is more difficult for short-faced dogs than it is for longer-muzzled dogs. Dogs with heart problems can also

> **CHIN HELD HIGH**
> Chin seem to have an inborn sense of self-esteem and dignity. They appear to have no sense whatsoever of inferiority and are deeply hurt by harsh discipline. Many owners say their Chin "pout," and they can certainly become depressed if they find themselves in a non-loving environment.

suffer in this way. It is therefore particularly important not to allow Chin to get too hot, such as they would if left in a car, even on a mild day! Heat stroke is highly dangerous and a frightening experience, so must be avoided at all costs.

Veterinary assistance should be sought immediately, but initially the dog should be kept quiet and as cool as possible, with cool (not cold) water applied to the head, neck, shoulders, belly and inside the legs. Run water over his mouth and tongue, but do not try to force him to drink if he will not. Do not delay in beginning this treatment and then getting him to the vet. It is always a sensible precaution to allow a Chin to travel with a non-spill water bowl in his travel crate; this way, at least he has access to a drink of water if he begins to feel the heat.

### Pinched Nostrils

Although the majority of Japanese Chin have large nostrils, a feature

Even lap dogs enjoy time in the great outdoors. Fresh air and sunshine are vital to the good health and genuine happiness of your Chin.

required in the breed standard, tight nostrils do appear in some and can lead to health problems. Nostrils that are tight can be apparent at birth but sometimes cannot be noticed until between 10 and 21 days of age. Since breeders would never sell a Chin puppy younger than 10 weeks of age, it should be clear whether or not the nostrils are affected before a transaction takes place.

### LONG HEAT CYCLES

Although not a health problem, it is worthy of mention that some Japanese Chin bitches have longer heat cycles (estrus) than seen in other dogs.

### UMBILICAL HERNIAS

An umbilical hernia, seen as a small swelling at the sight of the umbilicus, is not uncommon in the Chin. Such hernias can be hereditary or, possibly more frequently, caused by a bitch's tugging too forcefully on the umbilical cord.

Most hernias are entirely trouble-free, but if they become very hard or swollen it is wise to ask a vet to check the hernia, for sometimes surgical rectification is needed.

### SNORTING

Some Japanese Chin, like many other of the short-nosed breeds, suffer from snorting, caused by elongation of the soft palate. Although alarming for the novice owner, this is rarely a problem. The dog will usually stand four-square with sides heaving, but the problem will go away almost as soon as it came. To help alleviate the situation, it is a good idea to place your thumb over the dog's nose, causing the dog to breathe through its mouth, following which breathing will return to normal.

### OTHER HEALTH PROBLEMS

The main heart problems seen in the Japanese Chin are early-onset heart murmurs and congestive heart failure. Aside from patellar luxation, another orthopedic problem that can affect the breed is "roach back" (disc problems). Seizures have been cited in the Chin as well. Discuss these and all problems with your breeder to ensure that your pup comes from healthy stock and so that your Chin can have all of the proper exams to detect any problems as early as possible. Sometimes ongoing testing, such as annually or every few years, is advised for certain problems.

The Chin that goes home with the ribbon is the Chin that the judge believes to be closest to the breed standard. This is the premise upon which conformation dog shows are based.

# JAPANESE CHIN

## INTRODUCTION TO THE BREED STANDARD

A breed standard is a written description of what the ideal specimen of the breed should look like. The standard is used by judges and breeders alike as a sort of "blueprint" to guide in their assessment of quality in the breed. The standard defines the general appearance, characteristics, temperament and specific physical traits (such as head, mouth, body, tail), as well as size and gait (movement). The ineffable "type" of a breed is the attainable sum of the parts that the standard describes.

All breed standards are designed effectively to paint a picture in words, though each reader will almost certainly have a slightly different way of interpreting these words. After all, when all is said and done, were everyone to interpret a breed standard in exactly the same way, there would only be one consistent winner within the breed at any given time!

In any event, to fully comprehend the intricacies of a breed, reading words alone is never enough. In addition, it is essential for devotees to watch the Japanese

**MEETING THE IDEAL**

The American Kennel Club defines a standard as: "A description of the ideal dog of each recognized breed, to serve as an ideal against which dogs are judged at shows." This "blueprint" is drawn up by the breed's recognized parent club, approved by a majority of its membership, and then submitted to the AKC for approval. The AKC states that "An understanding of any breed must begin with its standard. This applies to all dogs, not just those intended for showing." The picture that the standard draws of the dog's type, gait, temperament and structure is the guiding image used by breeders as they plan their programs.

Chin being judged at shows and, if possible, to attend seminars at which the breed is discussed. This enables owners to absorb as much as possible about this delightful little breed. "Hands-on" experience, providing an opportunity to assess the structure of dogs, is always valuable, especially for those who hope ultimately to judge the breed.

A breed standard also functions to help breeders to produce stock that come as close as possible to the recognized standard, and helps judges to know exactly what they are looking for. This enables judges to make a carefully considered decision when selecting the most typical Chin to head their line of winners.

However familiar you are with the breed, it is always worth refreshing your memory by re-reading the standard, for it is sometimes all too easy to overlook, or perhaps conveniently forget, certain features.

## AMERICAN KENNEL CLUB BREED STANDARD FOR THE JAPANESE CHIN

**General Appearance:** The Japanese Chin is a small, well balanced, lively, aristocratic Toy dog with a distinctive Oriental expression. It is light and stylish in action. The plumed tail is carried over the back, curving to either side. The coat is profuse, silky, soft and straight. The dog's outline presents a square appearance.

**Size, Proportion, Substance:** *Size*—Ideal size is 8 inches to 11 inches at the highest point of the withers. *Proportion*—Length between the sternum and the buttock is equal to the height at the withers. *Substance*—Solidly built, compact, yet refined. Carrying good weight in proportion to height and body build.

**Head:** *Expression*—Bright, inquisitive, alert, and intelligent. The distinctive Oriental expression is characterized by the large broad head, large wide-set eyes, short broad muzzle, ear feathering and the evenly patterned facial markings. *Eyes*—Set wide apart, large, round, dark in color and lustrous. A small amount of white showing in the inner corners of the eyes is a breed characteristic that gives the dog a look of astonishment. *Ears*—Hanging, small, V-shaped, wide apart, set slightly below the crown of the skull. When alert, the ears are carried forward and downward. The ears are well feathered and fit into the rounded contour of the head. *Skull*—Large, broad, slightly rounded between the ears but not domed. Forehead is prominent, rounding toward the nose. Wide across the level of the eyes. In profile, the forehead and muzzle touch on the same vertical plane of a right angle whose horizontal plane is the top of the skull. *Stop*—Deep. *Muzzle*—Short and broad with well-cushioned cheeks and rounded upper lips that cover the teeth. *Nose*—Very short with wide, open nostrils. Set on a level with the middle of the eyes and upturned. Nose leather is black in the black and white and the black and white with tan points, and is self-colored or black in the red and white. *Bite*—The jaw is wide and slightly undershot. A dog with one or two missing or slightly misaligned teeth should not be severely penalized. The Japanese Chin is very sensitive to oral examination. If the dog displays any hesitancy, judges are asked to defer to the handler for presentation of the bite.

**Neck, Topline, Body:** *Neck*—Moderate in length and thickness. Well set on the shoulders enabling the dog to carry its head up proudly. *Topline*—Level. *Body*—Square, moderately wide in the chest with rounded ribs. Depth of rib extends to the elbow. *Tail*—Set on high, carried arched up over the back and flowing to either side of the body.

**Forequarters:** *Legs*—Straight, and fine boned, with the elbows set close to the body. Removal of dewclaws is optional. *Feet*—Hare-shaped with feathering on the ends of the toes in the mature dog. Point

straight ahead or very slightly outward.

**Hindquarters:** *Legs*—Straight as viewed from the rear and fine boned. Moderate bend of stifle. Removal of dewclaws is optional. *Feet*—Hare-shaped with feathering on the ends of the toes in the mature dog. Point straight ahead.

**Coat:** Abundant, straight, single, and silky. Has a resilient texture and a tendency to stand out from the body, especially on neck, shoulders, and chest areas where the hair forms a thick mane or ruff. The tail is profusely coated and forms a plume. The rump area is heavily coated and forms culottes or pants. The head and muzzle are covered with short hair except for

A Japanese Chin of correct type, balance and structure, with the correct coat.

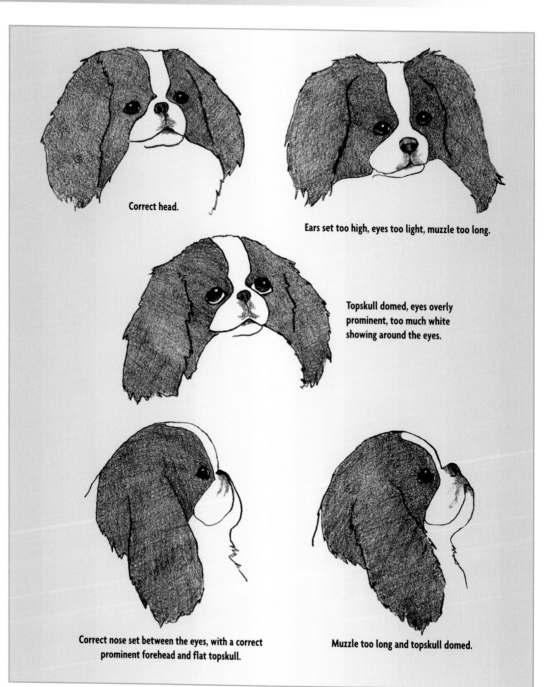

Correct head.

Ears set too high, eyes too light, muzzle too long.

Topskull domed, eyes overly prominent, too much white showing around the eyes.

Correct nose set between the eyes, with a correct prominent forehead and flat topskull.

Muzzle too long and topskull domed.

the heavily feathered ears. The forelegs have short hair blending into profuse feathering on the backs of the legs. The rear legs have the previously described culottes, and in mature dogs, light feathering from hock joint to the foot.

**Color:** Either black and white, red and white or black and white with tan points. The term tan points shall include tan or red spots over each eye, inside the ears, on both cheeks, and at the anal vent area if displaying any black. The term red shall include all shades of red, orange and lemon, and sable,

Low on leg and body too long.     Sparse coat, too fine-boned, weak pasterns and weak rear.

which includes any aforementioned shade intermingled or overlaid with black. Among the allowed colors there shall be no preference when judging. A clearly defined white muzzle and blaze are preferable to a solidly marked head. Symmetry of facial markings is preferable. The size, shape, placement or number of body patches is not of great importance. The white is clear of excessive ticking.

**Gait:** Stylish and lively in movement. Moves straight with front and rear legs following in the same plane.

**Temperament:** A sensitive and intelligent dog whose only purpose is to serve man as a companion. Responsive and affectionate with those it knows and loves but reserved with strangers or in new situations.

**Approved December 8, 1992**
**Effective January 27, 1993**

## THE CHIN'S GAIT

The desired movement of the Chin should be stylish and straight, befitting the breed's proud demeanor. The term "plaiting" refers to walking or trotting with the front legs crossing, which is undesirable in the Chin.

# JAPANESE CHIN

## HOW TO SELECT A PUPPY

Before reaching the decision that you will begin your search for a Japanese Chin puppy, it is essential that you are certain that this is the most suitable breed for you, your family and your lifestyle. You should have done plenty of background "homework" on the breed, including contacting the Japanese Chin Club of America for breed information and breeder referrals, and preferably have visited a few shows at which the breed was exhibited, giving you an opportunity to see the Japanese Chin in some numbers. This will also have provided you with a chance to see the dogs with their breeders and

Part of the fun and education of puppy selection is watching the litter play and interact together.

> **THE FAMILY TREE**
> Your puppy's pedigree is his family tree. Just as a child may resemble his parents and grandparents, so too will a puppy reflect the qualities, good and bad, of his ancestors, especially those in the first two generations. Therefore it's important to know as much as possible about a puppy's immediate relatives. Reputable and experienced breeders should be able to explain the pedigree and why they chose to breed from the particular dogs they used.

owners, which is important. Black and white Chin are more easily found than the other color varieties, and you may decide that you have a preference where color is concerned.

Remember that the dog you select should remain with you for the duration of its life, which should be well over a decade, so making the right decision from the outset is of the utmost importance. No dog should be moved from one home to another simply because his owners were not considerate enough to have

done sufficient background research before deciding on the Japanese Chin.

It is unlikely that you will find a large number of litters of Japanese Chin available for sale at any given time, which means you may have to put your name on a waiting list with the breeder of your choice. Likewise, Chin litters are quite small, often containing one to three puppies, further limiting availability. But always remember that, when looking for a puppy, a good breeder will be assessing you as a prospective new owner just as carefully as you are selecting the breeder.

Always be certain that the puppy that you finally choose has a stable, outgoing personality, expressing curiosity. Never take pity on an unduly shy puppy, for in doing so you will be asking for trouble in the long run. Such a dog is likely to have serious problems in socializing. Also remember that the Chin puppy that you select should not show any sign of aggression. Be on the lookout for deafness when purchasing a puppy, for deafness does occur occasionally in the breed. One that remains soundly asleep, not responding to sudden noise, may be suspect.

Puppies almost invariably look enchanting, but you must select one from a caring breeder who has given the puppies all the attention they deserve, and has

### SELECTING FROM THE LITTER

Before you visit a litter of puppies, promise yourself that you won't fall for the first pretty face you see! Decide on your goals for your puppy—show prospect, agility competitor, family companion—and then look for a puppy who displays the appropriate qualities. In most litters, there is an Alpha pup (the bossy puppy), and occasionally a shy fellow who is less confident, with the rest of the litter falling somewhere in the middle. "Middle-of-the-roaders" are safe bets for most families and novice competitors.

looked after them well. They should already have been well socialized, and this is likely to be apparent when you meet them. Never consider buying through a third party. You want to know exactly how your puppy was raised and to see the litter's dam, at least, though the sire may live many miles away. However, a good breeder will be able to show you his picture and pedigree, and to tell you all about him.

Since you are likely to be choosing a Japanese Chin as a pet dog and not a show dog, you simply should select a pup that is friendly, attractive and healthy. The puppy that you select should look well fed, but not pot-bellied, as this might indicate worms. Eyes should look bright and clear, without discharge. The nose should be moist, an indication of good health, but should never be runny. There should certainly be no evidence of loose motions or parasites. The puppy you choose should also have a healthy-looking coat, an important indicator of good health internally.

Grooming is a big part of life for Chin and owners, and something to which a pup should be introduced early in life.

> ### FINDING A QUALIFIED BREEDER
> Before you begin your puppy search, ask for references from your veterinarian and perhaps other breeders to refer you to someone they believe is reputable. Responsible breeders usually raise only one or two breeds of dog. Avoid any breeder who has several different breeds or has several litters at the same time. Dedicated breeders are usually involved with a breed or other dog club. Many participate in some sport or activity related to their breed. Just as you want to be assured of the breeder's qualifications, the breeder wants to be assured that you will make a worthy owner. Expect the breeder to interview you, asking questions about your goals for the pup, your experience with dogs and what kind of home you will provide.

Always check the bite of your selected puppy to be sure that it is developing correctly, as wry mouth is a problem in the Japanese Chin. The desired bite is slightly undershot. A wry mouth or a cross bite is highly undesirable, and common in some lines of Chin. In general, Chin are very sensitive about having their mouths handled. Even trained show dogs may not tolerate a stranger touching their mouths. Have the breeder show you the puppy's bite, and that of the dam

## SIGNS OF A HEALTHY PUPPY

Healthy puppies are robust little fellows who are alert and active, sporting shiny coats and supple skin. They should not appear lethargic, bloated or pot-bellied, nor should they have flaky skin or runny or crusted eyes or noses. Their stools should be firm and well formed, with no evidence of blood or mucus.

A young Chin is a tiny, precious creature that makes giant demands on his new owner. Are you ready to take this step?

as well. The correct bite is important for show dogs as well as pet dogs, as an improper bite can cause problems with eating.

In preparing to bring home a puppy, you may want to consider whether or not to take out veterinary insurance. Veterinary bills can mount up, and you must always be certain that sufficient funds are available to give your dog any veterinary attention that may be needed. Veterinary policies can be quite affordable, some even covering routine visits and vaccinations.

Breeders commonly allow visitors to see their litters by around the fifth or sixth week, and puppies leave for their new homes about the tenth to twelfth week. Due to the breed's daintiness and the tiny size of puppies, breeders should never allow pups to leave for new homes earlier than the tenth week. Likewise, Chin puppies receive better socialization if not removed any sooner than this, learning much from their dam and siblings as well. Qualified breeders spend significant amounts of time with the Japanese Chin toddlers so that the pups are able to interact with the "other species," i.e. humans. Given the long history that dogs and humans have, bonding between the two species is natural but must be nurtured. A well-

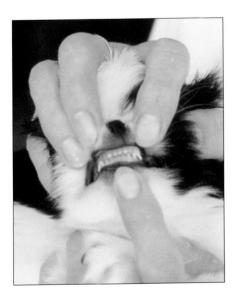

The desired bite is slightly undershot. Like most Toy dogs, Chins usually don't like their mouths handled, though show dogs must become accustomed to this inspection.

bred, well-socialized Japanese Chin pup wants nothing more than to be near you and please you.

## A COMMITTED NEW OWNER

By now you should understand what makes the Japanese Chin a most unique and special dog, one that will fit nicely into your family and lifestyle. If you have researched breeders, you should be able to recognize a knowledgeable and responsible Japanese Chin breeder who cares not only

*The typical Chin is bright, good-natured and responsive to training.*

### PEDIGREE VS. REGISTRATION CERTIFICATE

Too often new owners are confused between these two important documents. Your puppy's pedigree, essentially a family tree, is a written record of a dog's genealogy of three generations or more. The pedigree will show you the names as well as performance titles of all dogs in your pup's background. Your breeder must provide you with a registration application, with his part properly filled out. You must complete the application and send it to the AKC with the proper fee. Every puppy must come from a litter that has been AKC-registered by the breeder, born in the USA and from a sire and dam that are also registered with the AKC.

The seller must provide you with complete records to identify the puppy. The AKC requires that the seller provide the buyer with the following: breed; sex, color and markings; date of birth; litter number (when available); names and registration numbers of the parents; breeder's name; and date sold or delivered.

about his pups but also about what kind of owner you will be. If you have completed the final step in your new journey, you have found a litter, or possibly two, of quality Japanese Chin pups.

A visit with the puppies and their breeder should be an

education in itself. Breed research, breeder selection and puppy visitation are very important aspects of finding the puppy of your dreams. Beyond that, these things also lay the foundation for a successful future with your pup. Puppy personalities within each litter vary, from the shy and easygoing puppy to the one who is dominant and assertive, with most pups falling somewhere in between. By spending time with the puppies, you will be able to recognize certain behaviors and what these behaviors indicate about each pup's temperament. Which type of

A few inches can mean a significant difference in a small breed. While neither of these dogs is big, there is a noticeable variation in height.

pup will complement your family dynamics is best determined by observing the puppies in action within their "pack." Your breeder's expertise and recommendations are also valuable. Although you may fall in love with a bold and brassy male, the breeder may suggest that another pup would be best for you. The breeder's experience in rearing Japanese Chin pups and matching their temperaments with appropriate humans offers the best assurance that your pup will meet your needs and expectations. The type of puppy that you select is just as important as your decision that the Japanese Chin is the breed for you.

The decision to live with a Japanese Chin is a serious commitment and not one to be taken lightly. This puppy is a living sentient being that will be dependent on you for basic

## A SHOW PUPPY

If you plan to show your puppy, you must first deal with a reputable breeder who shows his dogs and has had some success in the conformation ring. The puppy's pedigree should include one or more champions in the first and second generation. You should be familiar with the breed and breed standard so you can know what qualities to look for in your puppy. The breeder's observations and recommendations also are invaluable aids in selecting your future champion. If you consider an older puppy, be sure that the puppy has been properly socialized with people and not isolated in a kennel without substantial daily human contact.

For the adult Chin, maintenance is easy with a complete and balanced food for small breeds and a constant supply of water.

survival for his entire life. Beyond the basics of survival—food, water, shelter and protection—he needs much, much more. The new pup needs love, nurturing and a proper canine education to mold him into a responsible, well-behaved canine citizen. Your Japanese Chin's health and good manners will need consistent monitoring and regular "tune-ups," so your job as a responsible dog owner will be ongoing throughout

### COST OF OWNERSHIP
The purchase price of your puppy is merely the first expense in the typical dog budget. Quality dog food, veterinary care (sickness and health maintenance), dog supplies and grooming costs will add up to big bucks every year. Can you adequately afford to support a canine addition to the family?

every stage of his life. If you are not prepared to accept these responsibilities and commit to them for the next decade, likely longer, then you are not prepared to own a dog of any breed.

Although the responsibilities of owning a dog may at times tax your patience, the joy of living with your Japanese Chin far outweighs the workload, and a well-mannered adult dog is worth your time and effort. Before your very eyes, your new charge will grow up to be your most loyal friend, devoted to you unconditionally.

### YOUR JAPANESE CHIN SHOPPING LIST
Just as expectant parents prepare a nursery for their baby, so should you ready your home for the arrival of your Japanese Chin pup. If you have the necessary puppy supplies purchased and in place before he comes home, it will ease the puppy's transition from the warmth and familiarity of his mom and littermates to the brand-new environment of his new home and human family. You will be too busy to stock up and prepare your house after your pup comes home, that's for sure! Imagine how a pup must feel upon being transported to a strange new place. It's up to you to comfort him and to let your little pup know that he is going to be happy with you!

## FOOD AND WATER BOWLS

Your puppy will need separate bowls for his food and water. Stainless steel pans are generally preferred over plastic bowls since they sterilize better and pups are less inclined to chew on the metal. Heavy-duty ceramic bowls are popular, but consider how often you will have to pick up those heavy bowls! You will only need small-sized bowls for your Chin as a puppy or adult.

### CRATE EXPECTATIONS

To make the crate more inviting to your puppy, you can offer his first meal or two inside the crate, always keeping the crate door open so that he does not feel confined. Keep a favorite toy or two in the crate for him to play with while inside. You can also cover the crate at night with a lightweight sheet to make it more den-like and remove the stimuli of household activity. Never put him into his crate as punishment or as you are scolding him, since he will then associate his crate with negative situations and avoid going there.

## THE DOG CRATE

If you think that crates are tools of punishment and confinement for when a dog has misbehaved, think again. Most breeders and almost all trainers recommend a crate as the preferred house-training aid as well as for all-around puppy training and safety. Because dogs are natural den creatures that prefer cave-like environments, the benefits of crate use are many. The crate provides the puppy with his very own "safe house," a cozy

Small, sturdy, easy-to-clean bowls are necessary for the Japanese Chin.

Breeders start their pups off on a good-quality food once the pups are fully weaned. Your breeder will be a helpful source of advice on feeding at all life stages.

place to sleep, take a break or seek comfort with a favorite toy; a travel aid to house your dog when on the road, at motels or at the vet's office; a training aid to help teach your puppy proper toileting habits; a place of solitude when non-dog people happen to drop by and don't want a lively puppy—or even a well-behaved adult dog—saying hello or begging for attention.

Your local pet shop will have crates suitable for the Japanese Chin. The Chin will not need a large crate to house him comfortably.

Crates come in several types, although the wire crate and the fiberglass airline-type crate are the most popular. Both are safe and your puppy will adjust to either one, so the choice is up to you. The wire crates offer better visibility for the pup as well as better ventilation. Many of the wire crates easily fold down for easy transport. The fiberglass crates, similar to those used by the airlines for animal transport, are sturdier and more den-like. However, the fiberglass crates do not collapse and are less ventilated than a wire crate, which can be problematic, especially in hot weather. Some of the newer crates are made of heavy plastic mesh; they are very lightweight and fold up into slim-line suitcases. However, a mesh crate might not be suitable for a pup with manic chewing habits.

The Chin usually reaches his full height by nine months of age. Purchase a crate that will accommodate an adult Japanese Chin. Even though adult Chin are still small dogs, a tiny puppy-sized crate will quickly become usless. A small crate, measuring about 16 inches high by 14 inches wide by 20 inches deep, will suit him nicely.

### BEDDING AND CRATE PADS

Your puppy will enjoy some type of soft bedding in his "room" (the crate), something he can snuggle into to feel cozy and secure. Old towels or blankets are good choices for a young pup, since he may (and probably will) have a toileting accident or two in the crate or decide to chew on the bedding material. Once he is fully trained and out of the early chewing stage, you can replace the puppy bedding with a permanent crate pad if you prefer. Crate pads and other dog beds run the gamut from inexpensive to high-end doggie-designer styles, but don't splurge on the good stuff until you are sure that your puppy is reliable and won't tear it up or make a mess on it.

### PUPPY TOYS

Just as infants and older children require objects to stimulate their minds and bodies, puppies need toys to entertain their curious

## CONFINEMENT

It is wise to keep your puppy confined to a small "puppy-proofed" area of the house for his first few weeks at home. Gate or block off a space near the door he will use for outdoor potty trips. Expandable baby gates are useful to create puppy's designated area. If he is allowed to roam through the entire house or even only several rooms, it will be more difficult to house-train him.

brains, wiggly paws and achy teeth. A fun array of safe doggie toys will help satisfy your puppy's chewing instincts and distract him from gnawing on the leg of your antique chair or your new leather sofa. Most puppy toys are cute and look as if they would be a lot of fun, but not all are necessarily safe or good for your puppy, so use caution when you go puppy-toy shopping.

Japanese Chin generally are not very active chewers, but caution is warranted whenever your dog is playing with a toy. Good "chewcifiers" are rubber and nylon bones, which come in sizes appropriate for all ages and breeds. Remember that small dogs have small mouths and teeth, so think safety first but don't offer your Chin a harder chew than he can handle. Be especially careful of natural bones, which can splinter or develop dangerous sharp edges; pups can easily swallow or choke on those bone splinters. Veterinarians often tell

The responsibility of owning one Chin is multiplied many times over when you consider adopting a whole pack. Since this breed is so gregarious and relatively easy to keep, the temptation to keep adding to the Chin clan is considerable.

## TEETHING TIME

All puppies chew. It's normal canine behavior. Chewing just plain feels good to a puppy, especially during the three- to five-month teething period when the adult teeth are breaking through the gums. Rather than attempting to eliminate such a strong natural chewing instinct, you will be more successful if you redirect it and teach your puppy what he may or may not chew. Correct inappropriate chewing with a sharp "No!" and offer him a chew toy, praising him when he takes it. Don't become discouraged. Chewing usually decreases after the adult teeth have come in.

of surgical nightmares involving bits of splintered bone, because in addition to the danger of choking, the sharp pieces can damage the intestinal tract.

Similarly, rawhide chews, while a favorite of most dogs and puppies, can be equally dangerous. Pieces of rawhide are easily swallowed after they get all gummy from chewing, and dogs have been known to choke on large pieces of ingested rawhide. Rawhide chews should be offered only when you can supervise the puppy.

Soft stuffed toys are special favorites of the Japanese Chin. They come in a wide variety of cute shapes and sizes; some look like little stuffed animals. Puppies love to shake them up and toss them about, or simply carry them around. Be careful of fuzzy toys that have button eyes or noses that your pup could chew off and swallow, and make sure that he does not disembowel a squeaky toy to remove the squeaker! Braided rope toys are similar in that they are fun to chew and toss around, but they shred easily and the strings are easy to swallow. The strings are not digestible and, if the puppy doesn't pass them in his stool, he could end up at the vet's office. As with rawhides, your puppy should be closely monitored with rope toys.

If you believe that your pup has ingested a piece of one of his toys, check his stools for the next couple of days to see if he passes the item when he defecates. At the same time, also watch for signs of intestinal distress. A call to your veterinarian might be in order to get his advice and be on the safe side.

An all-time favorite toy for puppies (young and old!) is the empty gallon milk jug. Hard plastic juice containers—46 ounces or more—are also excellent. Such containers make lots of noise when they are batted about, and puppies go crazy with delight as they play with them. However, they don't often last very long, so be sure to remove and replace them when they get chewed up.

A word of caution about homemade toys: be careful with your choices of non-traditional play objects. Never use old shoes or socks, since a puppy cannot distinguish between the old ones on which he's allowed to chew and the new ones in your closet that are strictly off-limits. That principle applies to anything that resembles something that you don't want your puppy to chew.

### COLLARS

A lightweight nylon collar is the best choice for a very young pup. Quick-clip collars are easy to put on and remove, and they can be adjusted as the puppy grows. Introduce him to his collar as

### TOYS 'R SAFE

The vast array of tantalizing puppy toys is staggering. Stroll through any pet shop or pet-supply outlet and you will see that the choices can be overwhelming. However, not all dog toys are safe or sensible. Most very young puppies enjoy soft woolly toys that they can snuggle with and carry around. (You know they have outgrown them when they shred them up!) Avoid toys that have buttons, tabs or other enhancements that can be chewed off and swallowed. Soft toys that squeak are fun, but make sure your puppy does not disembowel the toy and remove (and swallow) the squeaker. Toys that rattle or make noise can excite a puppy, but they present the same danger as the squeaky kind and so require supervision. Sturdy rubber toys that bounce can also entertain a pup, but make sure that the toy is too big for your pup to swallow.

Merchandise stands at dog shows offer a wide range of dog accessories from necessity to novelty for many breeds.

### LEASHES

A 6-foot nylon lead is an excellent choice for a young puppy. It is lightweight and not as tempting to chew as a leather lead. You can switch to a 6-foot leather lead after your pup has grown and is used to walking politely on a lead. For initial puppy walks and house-training purposes, you should invest in a shorter lead so that you have more control over the puppy. At first, you don't want him wandering too far away from you, and when taking him out for toileting you will want to keep him in the specific area chosen for his potty spot.

soon as he comes home to get him accustomed to wearing it. He'll get used to it quickly and won't mind a bit. Make sure that it is snug enough that it won't slip off, yet loose enough to be comfortable for the pup. You should be able to slip two fingers between the collar and his neck. Check the collar often, as puppies grow in spurts, and his collar can become too tight almost overnight. Choke collars should *never* be used with the Japanese Chin.

Once the puppy is heel trained with a traditional leash, you can consider purchasing a retractable lead. A retractable lead is excellent for walking adult dogs that are already leash-wise. This type of lead allows the dog to roam farther away from you and explore a wider area when out walking, and also retracts when you need to keep him close to you.

### SWEETS THAT KILL

Antifreeze would be every dog's favorite topping for a chocolate sundae! However, antifreeze, just like chocolate, kills dogs. Ethylene glycol, found in antifreeze, causes acute renal failure in dogs and can be fatal. Dogs suffering from kidney failure expel little or no urine, act lethargically, may experience vomiting or diarrhea and may resist activity and drinking water. Just a single teaspoon of antifreeze is enough to kill a dog (depending on the size); even for large dogs, it takes only a tablespoon or two! Like that irresistible but toxic chocolate, antifreeze is sweet-tasting and smells yummy. Keep both away from your dog!

# COLLARING OUR CANINES

The standard flat collar with a buckle or a snap, in leather, nylon or cotton, is widely regarded as the everyday all-purpose collar. If the collar fits correctly, you should be able to fit two fingers between the collar and the dog's neck.

**Leather Buckle Collars**

**Limited-Slip Collar**

The martingale, Greyhound or limited-slip collar is preferred by many dog owners and trainers. It is fixed with an extra loop that tightens when pressure is applied to the leash. The martingale collar gets tighter but does not "choke" the dog. The limited-slip collar should only be used for walking and training, not for free play or interaction with another dog. These types of collar should never be left on the dog, as the extra loop can lead to accidents.

Choke collars, usually made of stainless steel, are made for training purposes but are not recommended for small dogs or heavily coated breeds, and thus are unsuitable for the Chin. The chains can injure small dogs or damage long/abundant coats. Thin nylon choke leads are commonly used on show dogs while in the ring, though they are not practical for everyday use.

The harness, with two or three straps that attach over the dog's shoulders and around his torso, is a humane and safe alternative to the conventional collar. By and large, a well-made harness is virtually escape-proof. Harnesses are available in nylon and mesh and can be outfitted on most dogs, with chest girths ranging from 10 to 30 inches.

**Snap Bolt Choke Collar**

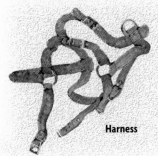

**Harness**

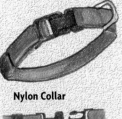

**Nylon Collar**

**Quick-Click Closure**

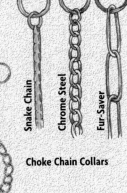

Snake Chain   Chrome Steel   Fur-Saver

**Choke Chain Collars**

A head collar, composed of a nylon strap that goes around the dog's muzzle and a second strap that wraps around his neck, offers the owner better control over his dog. This device is recommended for problem-solving with dogs (including jumping up, pulling and aggressive behaviors), but must be used with care.

A training halter, including a flat collar and two straps, made of nylon and webbing, is designed for walking. There are several on the market; some are more difficult to put on the dog than others. The halter harness, with two small slip rings at each end, is recommended for ease of use.

## HOME SAFETY FOR YOUR PUPPY

The importance of puppy-proofing cannot be overstated. In addition to making your house comfortable for your Japanese Chin's arrival, you also must make sure that your house is safe for your puppy before you bring him home. There are countless hazards in the owner's personal living environment that a pup can sniff, chew, swallow or destroy. Many are obvious; others are not. Do a thorough advance house check to remove or rearrange those things that could hurt your puppy, keeping any potentially dangerous items out of areas to which he will have access.

Electrical cords are especially dangerous, since puppies view them as irresistible chew toys. Unplug and remove all exposed cords or fasten them beneath a baseboard where the puppy cannot reach them. Veterinarians and firefighters can tell you horror stories about electrical burns and house fires that resulted from puppy-chewed electrical cords. Consider this a most serious precaution for your puppy and the rest of your family.

Scout your home for tiny objects that might be seen at a pup's eye level. Keep medication bottles and cleaning supplies well out of reach, and do the same with waste baskets and other trash containers. Check the house and

### THE GRASS IS ALWAYS GREENER

Must dog owners decide between their beloved canine pals and their perfectly manicured emerald-green lawns? Just as dog urine is no tonic for growing grass, lawn chemicals are extremely dangerous to your dog. Fertilizers, pesticides and herbicides pose real threats to canines and humans alike. Dogs should be kept off treated grounds for at least 24 hours following treatment. Consider some organic options for your lawn care, such as using a homemade compost or a natural fertilizer instead of a commercial chemical. Some dog-conscious lawnkeepers avoid fertilizers entirely, keeping up their lawns by watering, aerating, mowing and seeding frequently.

As always, dogs complicate the equation. Canines love grass. They roll in it, eat it and love to bury their noses in it—and then do their business in it! Grass can mean hours of feel-good, smell-good fun! In addition to the dangers of lawn-care chemicals, there's also the threat of burs, thorns and pebbles in the grass, not to mention the very common grass allergy. Many dogs develop an incurably itchy skin condition from grass, especially in the late summer when the world is in full bloom.

yard for plants toxic to dogs. It goes without saying that you should not use rodent poison or

# A Dog-Safe Home

The dog-safety police are taking you and your new puppy on a house tour. Let's go room by room and see how safe your own home is for your new pup. The following items are doggie dangers, so either they must be removed or the dog should be monitored or not allowed access to these areas.

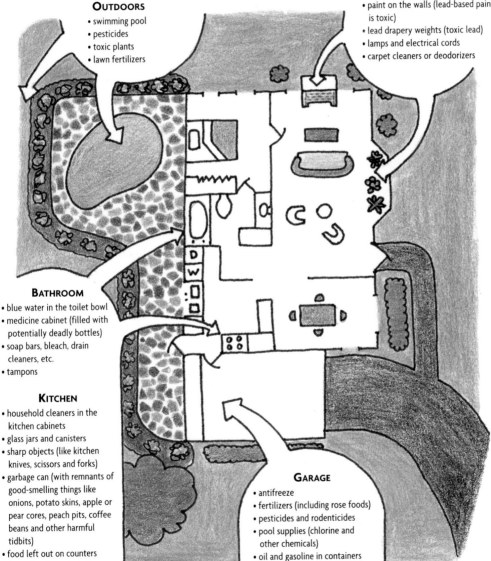

## Living Room
- house plants (some varieties are poisonous)
- fireplace or wood-burning stove
- paint on the walls (lead-based paint is toxic)
- lead drapery weights (toxic lead)
- lamps and electrical cords
- carpet cleaners or deodorizers

## Outdoors
- swimming pool
- pesticides
- toxic plants
- lawn fertilizers

## Bathroom
- blue water in the toilet bowl
- medicine cabinet (filled with potentially deadly bottles)
- soap bars, bleach, drain cleaners, etc.
- tampons

## Kitchen
- household cleaners in the kitchen cabinets
- glass jars and canisters
- sharp objects (like kitchen knives, scissors and forks)
- garbage can (with remnants of good-smelling things like onions, potato skins, apple or pear cores, peach pits, coffee beans and other harmful tidbits)
- food left out on counters (some foods are toxic to dogs)

## Garage
- antifreeze
- fertilizers (including rose foods)
- pesticides and rodenticides
- pool supplies (chlorine and other chemicals)
- oil and gasoline in containers
- sharp objects, electrical cords and power tools

option. Check the fence periodically for necessary repairs. If there is a weak link or space to squeeze through, you can be sure a determined Japanese Chin will discover it. Caution is always advised when the safety of your Chin is involved.

The garage and shed can be hazardous places for a pup, as things like fertilizers, chemicals and tools are usually kept there. It's best to keep these areas off-limits to the pup. Antifreeze is especially dangerous to dogs, as they find the taste appealing and it takes only a few drops from the driveway to kill a tiny Toy dog like the Chin.

*A snooping pup will investigate everything to which he has access, so don't let him follow his nose into danger.*

other toxic chemicals in any puppy area and that you must keep such containers safely locked up. You will be amazed at how many places a curious puppy can discover and you might be surprised at the places you find your Chin!

Once your house has cleared inspection, check your yard. A sturdy fence, well embedded into the ground, will give your dog a safe place to play and potty. Although Japanese Chin are not known to be fence jumpers or diggers, they still need a fence of adequate height, about 5 feet, to contain them. The Chin is more likely to climb a fence than to jump over or dig under, so a chain-link fence is not the best

**VISITING THE VETERINARIAN**
A good veterinarian with experience in Toy breeds is your Japanese Chin puppy's best health-insurance policy. If you do not already have a vet, ask friends and experienced dog people in your area for recommendations so that you can select a vet before you bring your Japanese Chin puppy home. Also arrange for your puppy's first veterinary examination beforehand, since many vets do not have appointments available right away, and your pup should visit the vet within a day or so of coming home.

It's important to make sure your puppy's first visit to the vet is a pleasant and positive one.

## PUPPY PARASITES

Parasites are nasty little critters that live in or on your dog or puppy. Most puppies are born with ascarid roundworms, which are acquired from dormant ascarids residing in the dam. Other parasites can be acquired through contact with infected fecal matter. Take a stool sample to your vet for testing. He will prescribe a safe wormer to treat any parasites found in your puppy's stool. Always have a fecal test performed at your puppy's annual veterinary exam.

The vet should take great care to befriend the pup and handle him gently to make their first meeting a positive experience. The vet will give the pup a thorough physical examination and set up a schedule for vaccinations and other necessary wellness visits. Be sure to show your vet any health and inoculation records, which you should have received from your breeder. Your vet is a great source of canine health information, so be sure to ask questions and take notes. Creating a health journal for your puppy will make a handy reference for his wellness and any future health problems that may arise.

### MEETING THE FAMILY

Your Japanese Chin's homecoming is an exciting time for all members of the family, and it's only natural that everyone will be eager to meet him, pet him and play with him. However, for the puppy's sake, it's best to make these initial family meetings as uneventful as possible so that the pup is not overwhelmed with too much too soon. Remember, he has just left his dam and his littermates and is away from the breeder's home for the first time. Despite his fuzzy wagging tail, he is still apprehensive and

Taking time to smell the flowers can be dangerous for a dog, as some plants are toxic to dogs or can be home to insects and allergens.

wondering where he is and who all these strange humans are. It's best to let him explore on his own and meet the family members as he feels comfortable. Let him investigate all the new smells, sights and sounds at his own pace. Children should be especially careful to handle the tiny Chin delicately, and not get overly excited or use loud voices. Be calm, gentle and affectionate, and be ready to comfort him if he appears frightened or uneasy.

Be sure to show your puppy his new crate during this first day home. Toss a treat or two inside the crate; if he associates the crate with food, he will associate the crate with good things. If he is comfortable with the crate, you

*Your pup's first night away from his familiar dam and littermates can be traumatic for the little one. Be reassuring and do not overwhelm the puppy with too much in his first few days in your home.*

**ESTABLISH A ROUTINE**
Routine is very important to a puppy's learning environment. To facilitate house-training, use the same exit/entrance door for potty trips and always take the puppy to the same place in the yard. The same principle of consistency applies to all other aspects of puppy training.

can offer him his first meal inside it. Leave the door ajar so he can wander in and out as he chooses.

**FIRST NIGHT IN HIS NEW HOME**
So much has happened in your Japanese Chin puppy's first day away from the breeder. He's had his first car ride to his new home. He's met his new human family and perhaps the other family pets. He has explored his new house and yard, at least those places where he is to be allowed during his first weeks at home. He may have visited his new veterinarian. He has eaten his first meal or two away from his dam and litter-mates. Surely that's enough to tire out a 12-week-old Japanese Chin pup...or so you hope!

It's bedtime. During the day, the pup investigated his crate, which is his new den and sleeping space, so it is not entirely strange to him. Line the crate with a soft towel or blanket that he can

Provide a cozy bed for your Chin puppy. If you let him snuggle with something brought from your puppy's former home, he will recognize the scent and may be comforted by this familiarity.

snuggle into and gently place him into the crate for the night. Some breeders send home a piece of bedding from where the pup slept with his littermates, and those familiar scents are a great comfort for the puppy on his first night without his siblings.

The Chin is a needy little one and, like all puppies, will whine. The puppy is objecting to the confinement and the fact that he is alone for the first time. This can be a stressful time for you as well as for the pup. It's important that you remain strong and don't let the puppy out of his crate to comfort him. He will fall asleep eventually. If you release him, the puppy will learn that crying means "out" and will continue that habit. You are laying the groundwork for future habits. Some breeders find that soft music can soothe a crying pup and help him get to sleep.

*Japanese Chin especially enjoy soft toys because they are fun to carry around and feel good to chew.*

## SOCIALIZING YOUR PUPPY

The first 20 weeks of your Japanese Chin puppy's life are the most important of his entire lifetime. A properly socialized puppy will grow up to be a confident and stable adult who will be a pleasure to live with and a welcome addition to the neighborhood.

The importance of socialization cannot be overemphasized. Research on canine behavior has proven that puppies who are not exposed to new sights, sounds, people and animals during their first 20 weeks of life will grow up to be timid and fearful, even aggressive, and unable to flourish outside of their familiar home environment.

Socializing your puppy is not difficult and, in fact, will be a fun time for you both. Lead training goes hand in hand with socialization, so your puppy will be learning how to walk on a lead at the same time that he's meeting the neighborhood. Because the Japanese Chin is a such a terrific breed, people will enjoy meeting "the new kid on the block." Take him for short walks, to the park and to other dog-friendly places where he will encounter new people, especially children. Puppies automatically recognize children as "little people" and are drawn to play with them. Just make sure that you supervise these meetings and that the children do not get too rough or encourage him to play too hard, as Chin are delicate as adults and especially fragile as puppies. Furthermore, an overzealous pup can often nip too hard, frightening the child and in turn making the puppy overly excited. A bad experience in puppyhood can impact a dog for life, so a pup that has a negative experience with a child may grow up to be shy or even aggressive around children.

Take your puppy along on

your daily errands. Puppies are natural "people magnets," and most people who see your pup will want to pet him. All of these encounters will help to mold him into a confident adult dog. Likewise, you will soon feel like a confident, responsible dog owner, rightly proud of your handsome Japanese Chin.

You will have acquired your Chin after the "fear period," which occurs during the eight- to ten-week-old period. This is a serious imprinting period, and all contact during this time should have been gentle and positive. A frightening or negative event could leave a permanent impression that could affect his future behavior if a similar situation arises.

Also make sure that your

puppy has received his first and second rounds of vaccinations before you expose him to other dogs or bring him to places that other dogs may frequent. Avoid dog parks and other strange-dog areas until your vet assures you that your puppy is fully immunized and resistant to the diseases that can be passed between canines. Discuss socialization with your breeder, as some breeders recommend socializing the puppy even before he has received all of his inoculations, depending on how outgoing the breed or puppy may be.

Play-fighting and roughhousing among the litter are normal behaviors as they posture for position in the puppy pack.

### BE CONSISTENT
Consistency is a key element, in fact is absolutely necessary, to a puppy's learning environment. A behavior (such as chewing, jumping up or climbing onto the furniture) cannot be forbidden one day and then allowed the next. That will only confuse the pup, and he will not understand what he is supposed to do. Just one or two episodes of allowing an undesirable behavior to "slide" will imprint that behavior on a puppy's brain and make that behavior more difficult to erase or change.

### LEADER OF THE PUPPY'S PACK
Like other canines, your puppy needs an authority figure, someone he can look up to and

regard as the leader of his "pack." His first pack leader was his dam, who taught him to be polite and not chew too hard on her ears or nip at her muzzle. He learned those same lessons from his litter-mates. If he played too rough, they cried in pain and stopped the game, which sent an important message to the rowdy puppy.

As puppies play together, they are also struggling to determine who will be the boss. Being pack animals, dogs need someone to be in charge. If a litter of puppies remained together beyond puppyhood, one of the pups would emerge as the strongest one, the one who calls the shots.

Once your puppy leaves the pack, he will look intuitively for a new leader. If he does not recognize you as that leader, he will try to assume that position for himself. Of course, it is hard to imagine your adorable Japanese Chin puppy trying to be in charge when he is so small and seemingly helpless. You must remember that these are natural canine instincts. Do not cave in and allow your pup to get the upper "paw"!

Just as socialization is so important during these first 20 weeks, so too is your puppy's early education. He was born without any bad habits. He does not know what is good or bad behavior. If he does things like

**A SMILE'S WORTH A MILE**
Don't embark on your puppy's training course when you're not in the mood. Never train your puppy if you're feeling grouchy or impatient with him. Subjecting your puppy to your bad mood is a bad move. Your pup will sense your negative attitude, and neither of you will enjoy the session or have any measure of success. Always begin and end your training sessions on a happy note.

nipping and digging, it's because he is having fun and doesn't know that humans consider these things as "bad." It's your job to teach him proper puppy manners, and this is the best time to accomplish that...before he has developed bad habits, since it is much more difficult to "unlearn" or correct unacceptable learned behavior than to teach good behavior from the start.

Make sure that all members of the family understand the importance of being consistent when training their new puppy. If you tell the puppy to stay off the sofa and your daughter allows him to cuddle on the couch with

If your Chin is introduced to other dogs and situations at a young age, you will have a dog that is comfortable with other dogs and calm in new environments.

her to watch her favorite TV show, your pup will be confused about what he is and is not allowed to do. Have a family conference before your pup comes home so that everyone understands the basic principles of puppy training and the rules you have set forth for the pup, and agrees to follow them.

The old saying that "an ounce of prevention is worth a pound of cure" is especially true when it comes to puppies. It is much easier to prevent inappropriate behavior than it is to change it. It's also easier and less stressful for the pup, since it will keep discipline to a minimum and create a more positive learning environment for him. That, in turn, will also be easier on you!

Here are a few commonsense tips to keep your belongings safe and your puppy out of trouble:

- Keep your closet doors closed and your shoes, socks and other apparel off the floor so your puppy can't get at them.
- Keep a secure lid on the trash container or put the trash where your puppy can't dig into it. He can't get into what's inaccessible to him!
- Supervise your puppy at all times to make sure he is not getting into mischief. If he starts to chew the corner of the

*Though Chin are not known to be chewers as compared to other dogs, all puppies enjoy chewing their way through the teething period.*

rug, you can distract him instantly by tossing a toy for him to fetch. You also will be able to whisk him outside when you notice that he is about to piddle on the carpet. If you can't see your puppy, you can't teach or correct his behavior.

**DOMESTIC SQUABBLES**

How well your new Japanese Chin will get along with an older dog who has squatter's rights depends largely on the individual dogs. Like people, some dogs are more gregarious than others and will enjoy having a furry friend to play with. Others will not be thrilled at the prospect of sharing their dog space with another canine.

It's best to introduce the dogs to each other on neutral ground, away from home, so the resident dog won't feel so possessive. You also want to make sure that a larger dog is not rough with your tiny Chin pup. Keep both puppy and adult on loose leads (loose is very important, as a tight lead

sends negative signals and can intimidate either dog) and allow them to sniff and do their doggy things. A few raised hackles are normal, with the older dog pawing at the youngster. Let the two work things out between them unless you see signs of real aggression, such as deep growls or curled lips and serious snarls. You may have to keep them separated until the veteran gets used to the new family member, often after the pup has outgrown the silly puppy stage and is more mature in stature. Take precautions to make sure that the puppy does not become frightened by the older dog's behavior.

Whatever happens, it's important to make your resident dog feel secure. (Jealousy is normal among dogs, too!) Pay extra attention to the older dog: feed him first, hug him first and don't insist he share his toys or space with the new pup until he's ready. If the two are still at odds months later, consult an obedience professional for advice.

Cat introductions are easier, believe it or not. Being agile and independent creatures, cats will scoot to high places, out of the puppy's reach. A cat might even tease the puppy and cuff him from above when the pup comes within paw's reach. However, most will end up buddies if you just let dog-and-cat nature run its course.

A crate-trained Chin will welcome time to himself in his crate, surrounded by his favorite toys. Crates are invaluable tools in house-training and safety, as well as acclimating the dog to his home.

# JAPANESE CHIN

Adding a Japanese Chin to your household means adding a new family member who will need your care each and every day. When your Japanese Chin pup first comes home, you will start a routine with him so that, as he grows up, your dog will have a daily schedule just as you do. The aspects of your dog's daily care will likewise become regular parts of your day, so you'll both have a new schedule. Dogs learn by consistency and thrive on routine: regular times for meals, exercise, grooming and potty trips are just as important for your dog as they are to you! Your dog's schedule will depend much on your family's daily routine, but remember that you now have a new member of the family who is part of your day every day!

## FEEDING

Feeding your dog the best diet is based on various factors, including age, activity level, overall condition and size of breed. When you visit the breeder, he will share with you his advice about the proper diet for your dog based on his experience with the breed and the foods with which he has had success. Likewise, your vet will be a helpful source of advice throughout the dog's life and will aid you in planning a diet for optimal health.

## FEEDING THE PUPPY

Of course, your pup's very first food will be his dam's milk. There

**NOT HUNGRY?**
No dog in his right mind would turn down his dinner, would he? If you notice that your dog has lost interest in his food, there could be any number of causes. Dental problems are a common cause of appetite loss, one that is often overlooked. If your dog has a toothache, a loose tooth or sore gums from infection, chances are it doesn't feel so good to chew. Think about when you've had a toothache! If your dog does not approach the food bowl with his usual enthusiasm, look inside his mouth for signs of a problem. Whatever the cause, you'll want to consult your vet so that your chow hound can get back to his happy, hungry self as soon as possible.

may be special situations in which pups fail to nurse, necessitating that the breeder hand-feed them with a formula, but, for the most part, pups spend the first weeks of life nursing from their dam. The breeder weans the pups by gradually introducing solid foods and decreasing the milk meals. Pups may even start themselves off on the weaning process, albeit inadvertently, if they snatch bites from their mom's food bowl.

By the time the pups are ready for new homes, they are fully weaned and eating a good puppy food. As a new owner, you may be thinking, "Great! The breeder has taken care of the hard part." Not so fast.

A puppy's first year of life is the time when all or most of his growth and development takes place. This is a delicate time, and diet plays a huge role in proper skeletal and muscular formation. Improper diet and exercise habits can lead to damaging problems that will compromise the dog's health and movement for his entire life. That being said, new owners should not worry needlessly. With the myriad types of food formulated specifically for growing pups of different-sized breeds, dog-food manufacturers have taken much of the guesswork out of feeding your puppy well. Since growth-food formulas are designed to provide the nutrition

## SWITCHING FOODS

There are certain times in a dog's life when it becomes necessary to switch his food; for example, from puppy to adult food and then from adult to senior-dog food. Additionally, you may decide to feed your pup a different type of food from what he received from the breeder, and there may be "emergency" situations in which you can't find your dog's normal brand and have to offer something else temporarily. Anytime a change is made, for whatever reason, the switch must be done gradually. You don't want to upset the dog's stomach or end up with a picky eater who refuses to eat something new. A tried-and-true approach is, over the course of about a week, to mix a little of the new food in with the old, increasing the proportion of new to old as the days progress. At the end of the week, you'll be feeding his regular portions of the new food, and he will barely notice the change.

that a growing puppy needs, it is unnecessary and, in fact, can prove harmful to add supplements to the diet. Research has shown that too much of certain vitamin supplements and minerals predispose a dog to skeletal problems. It's by no means a case of "if a little is good, a lot is better." At every stage of your dog's life, too much or too little in the way of nutrients can be harmful, which is why a manufactured complete food is the easiest way to know that your dog is getting what he needs.

Because of a young pup's small body and accordingly small digestive system, his daily portion will be divided up into small meals throughout the day. This can mean starting off with three or more meals a day and decreasing the number of meals as the pup matures. It is generally thought

*Gather round! Once the weaning process is complete, the breeder offers solid foods so that the pup is eating a complete puppy food when it's time to go to his new home.*

> **GRAPES & NUTS**
> Small amounts of fresh grapes and raisins can cause vomiting and diarrhea in dogs, possibly even kidney failure in the worst cases. Nuts, in general, are not recommended for dogs. Macadamia nuts, for example, can cause vomiting, diarrhea, fatigue and temporary paralysis of rear legs. Dogs usually recover from these symptoms in a few days. Almonds are also especially problematic for dogs.

that dividing the day's food into two meals on a morning/evening schedule is healthier for the dog's digestion, remembering that no dog should be fed immediately before or after exercise.

Regarding the feeding schedule, feeding the pup at the same times and in the same place each day is important for both housebreaking purposes and establishing the dog's everyday routine. As for the amount to feed, growing puppies generally need proportionately more food per body weight than their adult counterparts, but a pup should never be allowed to gain excess weight. Dogs of all ages should be kept in proper body condition, but extra weight can strain a pup's developing frame, causing skeletal problems.

Watch your pup's weight as he grows and, if the recommended amounts seem to be too much or too little for your pup, consult the vet about appropriate dietary changes. Keep in mind that treats, although small, can quickly add up throughout the day, contributing unnecessary calories. Treats are fine when used prudently; opt for dog treats specially formulated to be healthy or for nutritious snacks like small pieces of cheese or cooked chicken. If feeding dry dog biscuits, they should be broken up into small pieces to make it easier for your Chin's small mouth to handle.

### Feeding the Adult Dog

For the adult (meaning physically mature) dog, feeding properly is about maintenance, not growth. The Japanese Chin reaches full height as early as nine months of age, but continues filling out for longer. Since Chin are fairly active, they tend to do well on a higher protein diet. Under a vet's advisement, some owners like to supplement their Chins' dry food with some fresh protein in the form of small pieces of heart, chicken, lamb or minced meat. Again, correct weight is a concern. Your dog should appear fit and should have an evident "waist." His ribs should not be protruding (a sign of being underweight), but they should be covered by only a slight layer of fat. Under normal circumstances, an adult dog can be maintained fairly easily with a

**WEIGHT AND SEE!**
When you look at yourself in the mirror each day, you get very used to what you see! It's only when you pull out last year's holiday outfit and can't zip it up that you notice that you've put on some pounds. It's the same with dogs! Often a few pounds go unnoticed, and it's not until some time passes or the vet remarks that your dog looks more than pleasantly plump that you realize what's happened. To avoid your pet's becoming obese right under your very nose, make a habit of routinely evaluating his condition with a hands-on test.

Can you feel, but not see, your dog's rib cage? Does your dog have a waist? His waist should be evident by touch and also visible from above and from the side. In top view, the dog's body should have an hourglass shape. These are indicators of good condition. While it's not hard to spot an extremely skinny or overly rotund dog, it's the subtle changes that lead up to under- or overweight condition of which we must be aware. If your dog's ribs are visible, he is too thin. Conversely, if you can't feel the ribs under too much fat, and if there's no indication of a waistline, your dog is overweight. With a long-coated breed, these changes are often more easily felt than seen, so use the "hands-on" method with your Chin. Both of these conditions require changes to the diet. A trip or sometimes just a call to the vet will help you modify your dog's feeding.

high-quality nutritionally complete adult-formula food.

Factor treats into your dog's overall daily caloric intake, and avoid offering table scraps. It only takes a small amount of a toxic "people food" to damage a small dog; you also do not want to encourage begging and overeating.

## DIET DON'TS
- Got milk? Don't give it to your dog! Dogs cannot tolerate large quantities of cows' milk, as they do not have the enzymes to digest lactose.
- You may have heard of dog owners who add raw eggs to their dogs' food for a shiny coat or to make the food more palatable, but consumption of raw eggs too often can cause a deficiency of the vitamin biotin.
- Avoid feeding table scraps, as they will upset the balance of the dog's complete food. Additionally, fatty or highly seasoned foods can cause upset canine stomachs.
- Do not offer raw meat to your dog. Raw meat can contain parasites; it also is high in fat.
- Vitamin A toxicity in dogs can be caused by too much raw liver, especially if the dog already gets enough vitamin A in his balanced diet, which should be the case.
- Bones like chicken, pork chop and other soft bones are not suitable, as they easily splinter.

Overweight dogs are more prone to health problems. Research has even shown that obesity takes years off a dog's life. With that in mind, resist the urge to overfeed and over-treat. Don't make unnecessary additions to your dog's diet, whether with tidbits or with extra vitamins and minerals.

The amount of food needed for proper maintenance will vary depending on the individual dog's activity level, but you will be able to tell whether the daily portions are keeping him in good shape. With the wide variety of good complete foods available, choosing what to feed is largely a matter of personal preference. Just as with the puppy, the adult dog should have consistency in his mealtimes and feeding place. In addition to a consistent routine, regular mealtimes also allow the owner to see how much his dog is eating. If the dog seems never to be satisfied or, likewise, becomes uninterested in his food, the owner will know right away that something is wrong and can consult the vet.

### DIETS FOR THE AGING DOG
A good rule of thumb is that once a dog has reached 75% of his expected lifespan, he has reached "senior citizen" or geriatric status. Your Japanese Chin will be considered a senior at about 7–8 years of age; he has a projected lifespan of about 10–12 years.

## HOLD THE ONIONS

Sliced, chopped or grated; dehydrated, boiled, fried or raw; pearl, Spanish, white or red: onions can be deadly to your dog. The toxic effects of onions in dogs are cumulative for up to 30 days. A serious form of anemia, called Heinz body anemia, affects the red blood cells of dogs that have eaten onions. For safety (and better breath), dogs should avoid chives and scallions as well.

What does aging have to do with your dog's diet? No, he won't get a discount at the local diner's early-bird special. Yes, he will require some dietary changes to accommodate the changes that come along with increased age. One change is that the older dog's dietary needs become more similar to that of a puppy. Specifically, dogs can metabolize more protein as youngsters and seniors than in the adult-maintenance stage. Discuss with your vet whether you need to switch to a higher-protein or senior-formulated food or whether your current adult-dog food contains sufficient nutrition for the senior. If the senior Chin has dental problems or even missing teeth, which can happen in older dogs, soaking his dry food in water before feeding will make it easier for him to chew.

Watching the dog's weight remains essential, even more so in the senior stage. Older dogs are already more vulnerable to illness, and obesity only contributes to their susceptibility to problems. As the older dog becomes less active and, thus, exercises less, his regular portions may cause him to gain weight. At this point, you may consider decreasing his daily food intake or switching to a reduced-calorie food. As with other changes, you should consult your vet for advice.

### TYPES OF FOOD AND READING THE LABEL

When selecting the type of food to feed your dog, it is important to check out the label for ingredients. Many dry-food products have soybean, corn or rice as the main ingredient. The main ingredient will be listed first on the label,

Although your Chin's ancestors feasted at the table of noblemen, your Chin doesn't need to be spoiled by eating human foods.

Consider your
Chin's small
mouth and teeth
as a puppy and
adult when
choosing a food
that will be easy
for him to handle.

with the rest of the ingredients following in descending order according to their proportion in the food. While these types of dry food are fine, you should also look into dry foods based on meat or fish. These are better-quality foods and thus higher priced. However, they may be just as economical in the long run, because studies have shown that it takes less of the higher-quality foods to maintain a dog.

Comparing the various types of food, dry, canned and semi-moist, dry foods contain the least amount of water and canned foods the most. Proportionately, dry foods are the most calorie- and nutrient-dense, which means that you need more of a canned food product to supply the same amount of nutrition. In households with breeds of different size, the canned/dry/

semi-moist question can be of special importance. Larger breeds obviously eat more than smaller ones and thus in general do better on dry foods, but smaller breeds do fine on canned foods and require "small bite" formulations to protect their small mouths and teeth if fed only dry foods. "Small bite" foods are definitely recommended for the Chin. So if you have breeds of different sizes in your household, consider both your own preferences and what your dogs like to eat, but, as a rule, think canned for the little guys and dry or semi-moist for everyone else. You may find success mixing the food types or moistening your Chin's dry food. Water is important for all dogs, but even more so for those fed dry foods, as there is no high water content in their food.

There are strict controls that regulate the nutritional content of dog food, and a food has to meet the minimum requirements in order to be considered "complete and balanced." It is important that you choose such a food for your dog, so check the label to be sure that your chosen food meets the requirements. If not, look for a food that clearly states on the label that it is formulated to be complete and balanced for your dog's particular stage of life.

Recommendations for amounts to feed will also be indicated on the label. You should also ask your vet about proper food portions, and you will keep an eye on your dog's condition to see whether the recommended amounts are adequate. If he becomes over- or underweight, you will need to make adjustments; this also would be a good time to consult your vet.

The food label may also make feeding suggestions. Sometimes a splash of water will make the food more palatable for the dog and even enhance the flavor. Don't be overwhelmed by the many factors that go into feeding your dog. Manufacturers of complete and balanced foods make it easy, and once you find the right food and amounts for your Japanese Chin, his daily feeding will be a matter of routine.

### Don't Forget the Water!
For a dog, it's always time for a drink! Regardless of what type of food he eats, there's no doubt that he needs plenty of water. Fresh cold water, in a clean bowl, should be freely available to your dog at all times. There are special circumstances, such as during puppy housebreaking, when you will want to monitor your pup's water intake so that you will be able to predict when he will need to relieve himself, but water must be available to him nonetheless. Water is essential for hydration and proper body function just as it is in humans.

You will get to know how much your dog typically drinks in a day. Of course, in the heat or if exercising vigorously, he will be more thirsty and will drink more. However, if he begins to drink noticeably more water for no apparent reason, this could signal any of various problems, and you are advised to consult your vet.

Water is the best drink for dogs. Some owners are tempted to give milk from time to time or to moisten dry food with milk, but dogs do not have the enzymes necessary to digest the lactose in milk, which is much different from the milk that nursing puppies receive. Therefore, stick with clean fresh water to quench your dog's thirst, and always have it readily available to him.

### EXERCISE FOR YOUR CHIN
Although Japanese Chin are small, they are active dogs and thus

A constant supply of clean cold, fresh water is just as important as balanced nutrition.

**PUPPY STEPS**

Puppies are brimming with activity and enthusiasm. It seems that they can play all day and night without tiring, but don't overdo your puppy's exercise regimen. Easy does it for the puppy's first six to nine months. Keep walks brief and don't let the puppy engage in stressful jumping games. The puppy frame is delicate, and too much exercise during those critical growing months can cause injury to his bone structure, ligaments and musculature. Save his first jog for his first birthday!

the home or yard that might be dangerous, and be sure the yard is securely enclosed.

**GROOMING**

Despite the long coat, it is not especially difficult to keep a Japanese Chin in good condition. Even as a young puppy, your Chin should gain experience with grooming, so gentle brushing from just a few weeks of age will help to accustom him to the experience. Chin are usually groomed on a table with a non-slip surface, but do take care that they cannot jump off and injure themselves, especially if the leash is attached to the grooming table. Your Chin will very soon learn to associate the grooming table with a pleasurable experience to be shared with his owner. It is also a good idea to teach your Chin to lie on his back, and it is not unusual to see a pet Chin lying upside down on his owner's lap, enjoying a gentle brush.

thoroughly enjoy exercise. Adults will usually be more than happy to be taken for lead walks and will also enjoy free runs, though owners should be careful that the areas in which their dogs exercise are thoroughly safe. Because of Japanese Chin's diminutive size, it is only sensible for owners to be observant about which dogs they are likely to encounter, for often Chin don't seem to worry about which dogs they approach, and not all the dogs they meet will be friendly!

Provided a Chin lives in a home with a fenced yard, he will exercise himself quite happily in his home environment, especially if more than one dog is kept in the family. However, take care that your inquisitive Chin does not have access to anything around

Understandably, every owner has his own personal preference as to the best grooming equipment to use, but many people consider a pure bristle brush to be gentler to the coat than what is generally called a pinbrush. Many owners manage perfectly well using a stiff bristle brush on the ears, but others like to use a slicker brush instead, especially when removing mats. You will also need steel combs, both wide- and fine-toothed. When you are used to grooming your dog, you will find the type of equipment that you feel you can work with best. Initially, you will hopefully find that the breeder of your puppy will show you what grooming equipment he favors.

When grooming the head and ears, it is important to cover your Chin's eyes with your finger or thumb, so as to avoid accidental injury to the eye if the dog turns around suddenly. Always be careful whenever grooming around any dog's face.

If not groomed with some regularity, mats can form in the coat, especially behind the ears. When discovered, which is hopefully before they get too big and troublesome, they should be teased out with your fingers, always working from the skin outward. If you start pulling from the coat in towards the skin, you will simply succeed in making the knot even tighter. Some owners like to use a powder to aid the process, while others are happier just to use a conditioning spray or even a very light solution of water mixed with conditioner. This will help to prevent coat breakage, but always remember that when showing a dog, there should be no artificial substances in the coat when the dog enters the show ring.

After any mats have been carefully removed, brushing should be done in small areas at a time, until the entire coat has been done. It is common to do this

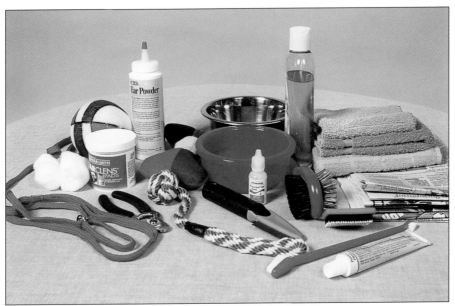

You will need good-quality grooming equipment to maintain your Chin's coat, as well as products for "housekeeping" tasks like cleaning eyes and ears and brushing teeth.

The Chin's tail is one of the breed's hallmarks and should be brushed and detangled with care to enhance the tail's characteristic "chrysanthemum" look.

in layers, brushing initially away from the direction of coat growth, then back into position again. A wide-toothed comb can then be used to put the finishing touches to the body coat, while a fine-toothed comb can be used on legs and ears. A final spray with a suitable coat conditioner is usually applied to finish the coat.

### NAILS AND FEET

Never forget that toenails should be kept short. If your dog walks on hard surfaces, nails will need less attention than the nails of dogs that walk primarily on soft surfaces. Canine nail clippers can easily be obtained from pet shops, and many owners find those of the "guillotine" design easiest to use.

Also check frequently between the pads to see that nothing has become trapped and needs to be removed. Great care must be taken not to damage the pads in the process.

### EYE AND EAR CARE

Eyes should always be kept clean and free from debris, by wiping the areas around the eyes with a clean moist cotton pad. Ears should also be checked regularly to see that they are clean and do not have an unpleasant smell, an indication of infection within the ear. Many good ear-cleaning formulas are now available, but take care not to probe into the ear canal, as this might cause injury. Use a cotton pad or cotton ball rather than poking around with a cotton swab.

### TEETH

Teeth should always be kept as free from tartar as possible in between your dog's veterinary dental exams which should take place at his regular check-up. There are now canine tooth-cleaning agents available, including the basics, like small toothbrushes and canine toothpaste. Since Toy dogs typically have problematic teeth, regular maintenance is critical for your Japanese Chin's mouth.

## WATER SHORTAGE

Pet shops sell excellent products, in both powder and spray forms, designed for spot-cleaning your dog. These dry shampoos are convenient for touch-up jobs when you don't have the time to bathe your dog in the traditional way. Muddy feet, messy behinds and smelly coats can be spot-cleaned and deodorized with a "wet-nap"-style cleaner. On those days when your dog insists on rolling in fresh goose droppings and there's no time for a bath, a spot bath can save the day. These pre-moistened wipes are also handy for other grooming needs like wiping faces, ears and eyes and freshening tails and behinds.

The slicker brush is preferred by some groomers for use around the Chin's ears, to help in removing mats.

A bristle brush is gentler for a thorough brushing of the body coat.

The coat and feathering are less likely to mat if you brush the dog every day.

Use a soft wipe and an ear-cleaning formula to keep your Chin's ears clean. Report any suspicious odors or evidence of parasites to your vet immediately.

Since Toy dogs commonly suffer from poor dentition and missing teeth, care of the Chin's teeth is vital to keep the dog's teeth in the best possible health.

The guillotine-type clippers are preferred by most dog groomers, as they are efficient and easiest to use.

## BATHING

In general, dogs need to be bathed only a few times a year, possibly more often if your dog gets into something messy or if he starts to smell like a dog. Show dogs are usually bathed before every show, which could be as frequent as weekly, although this depends on the owner. Bathing too frequently can have negative effects on the skin and coat, removing natural oils and causing dryness.

If you give your dog his first bath when he is young, he will become accustomed to the process. Wrestling a dog into the tub or chasing a freshly

shampooed dog who has escaped from the bath will be no fun! Most dogs don't naturally enjoy their baths, but you at least want yours to cooperate with you.

Before bathing the dog, have the items you'll need close at hand. First, decide where you will bathe the dog. You should have a tub or basin with a non-slip surface. Small dogs can even be bathed in a sink. In warm weather, some like to use a portable pool in the yard, although you'll want to make sure your dog doesn't head for the nearest dirt pile following his bath! You will also need a hose or shower spray to wet the coat thoroughly, a shampoo formulated for dogs, absorbent towels and a blow dryer, either one made for dogs or your own on a cool setting. Human shampoos are too harsh for dogs' coats and will dry them out.

Before wetting the dog, give

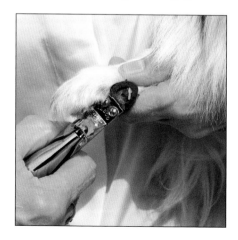

## SCOOTING HIS BOTTOM

Here's a doggy problem that many owners tend to neglect. If your dog is scooting his rear end around the carpet, he probably is experiencing anal-sac impaction or blockage. The anal sacs are the two grape-sized glands on either side of the dog's vent. The dog cannot empty these glands, which become filled with a foul-smelling material. The dog may attempt to lick the area to relieve the pressure. He may also rub his anus on your walls, furniture or floors.

Don't neglect your dog's rear end during grooming sessions. By squeezing both sides of the anus with a soft cloth, you can express some of the material in the sacs. If the material is pasty and thick, you likely will need the assistance of a veterinarian. Vets know how to express the glands and can show you how to do it correctly without hurting the dog or spraying yourself with the unpleasant liquid.

him a brush-through to remove any dead hair, dirt and mats. Make sure he is at ease in the tub and have the water at a comfortable temperature. Begin bathing by wetting the coat all the way down to the skin. Massage in the shampoo, keeping it away from his face and eyes. Rinse him thoroughly, again avoiding the eyes and ears, as you don't want to get water into the ear canals. A thorough rinsing is important, as shampoo residue is drying and itchy to the dog. After rinsing, wrap him in a towel to absorb the initial moisture. You can finish drying with either a towel or a blow dryer on low heat, held at a safe distance from the dog and brushing through the coat as you dry. You should keep the dog indoors and away from drafts until he is completely dry.

### ID FOR YOUR DOG

You love your Japanese Chin and want to keep him safe. Of course, you take every precaution to prevent his escaping from the yard or becoming lost or stolen. You have a sturdy high fence and you always keep your dog on-lead when out and about in public places. If your dog is not properly identified, however, you are overlooking a major aspect of his safety. We hope to never be in a situation where our dog is missing, but we should practice prevention in the unfortunate case that this happens; identification greatly increases the chances of your dog's being returned to you.

There are several ways to identify your dog. First, the traditional dog tag should be a staple in your dog's wardrobe, attached to his everyday collar. Tags can be made of sturdy plastic and various metals and should include your contact information so that a person who finds the dog

**PET OR STRAY?**
Besides the obvious benefit of providing your contact information to whoever finds your lost dog, an ID tag makes your dog more approachable and more likely to be recovered. A strange dog wandering the neighborhood without a collar and tags will look like a stray, while the collar and tags indicate that the dog is someone's pet. Even if the ID tags become detached from the collar, the collar alone will make a person more likely to pick up the dog.

can get in touch with you right away to arrange his return. Many people today enjoy the wide range of decorative tags available, so have fun and create a tag to match your dog's personality. Of course, it is important that the tag stays on the collar, so have a secure "O" ring attachment; you also can explore the type of tag that slides right onto the collar.

In addition to the ID tag, which every dog should wear even if identified by another method, two other forms of identification

have become popular: microchipping and tattooing. In microchipping, a tiny scannable chip is painlessly inserted under the dog's skin. The number is registered to you so that, if your lost dog turns up at a clinic or shelter, the chip can be scanned to retrieve your contact information.

The advantage of the microchip is that it is a permanent form of ID, but there are some factors to consider. Several different companies make microchips, and not all are compat-

If the need arises for you to board your Chin while on vacation, check out boarding kennels well in advance, making sure to find one that caters to small breeds, so you know you will be comfortable leaving your Chin in the kennel's care.

ible with the others' scanning devices. It's best to find a company with a universal microchip that can be read by scanners made by other companies as well. It won't do any good to have the dog chipped if the information cannot be retrieved. Also, not every humane society, shelter and clinic is equipped with a scanner, although more and more facilities are equipping themselves. In fact, many shelters microchip dogs that they adopt out to new homes.

In the US, there are five or six major microchip manufacturers as well as a few databases. The American Kennel Club's Companion Animal Recovery unit works in conjunction with HomeAgain™ Companion Animal Retrieval System (Schering-Plough). In the UK, The Kennel Club is affiliated with the National Pet Register, operated by Wood Green Animal Shelters.

Because the microchip is not visible to the eye, the dog must wear a tag that states that he is microchipped so that whoever picks him up will know to have him scanned. He of course also should have a tag with contact information in case his chip cannot be read. Humane societies and veterinary clinics offer this service, which is usually very affordable.

Though less popular than microchipping, tattooing is another permanent method of ID for dogs.

**CAR CAUTION**

You may like to bring your canine companion along on the daily errands, but if you will be running in and out from place to place and can't bring him indoors with you, leave him at home. Your dog should never be left alone in the car, not even for a minute—never! A car can heat up very quickly in any kind of weather, and even a cracked-open window will not help. In fact, leaving the window cracked will be dangerous if the dog becomes uncomfortable and tries to escape. When in doubt, leave your dog home, where you know he will be safe.

Most vets perform this service, and there are also clinics that perform dog tattooing. This is also an affordable procedure and one that will not cause much discomfort for the dog. It is best to put the tattoo in a visible area, such as the ear, to deter theft. It is sad to say that there are cases of dogs' being stolen and sold to research laboratories, but such laboratories will not accept tattooed dogs.

To ensure that the tattoo is effective in aiding your dog's return to you, the tattoo number must be registered with a national organization. That way, when someone finds a tattooed dog a phone call to the registry will quickly match the dog with his owner.

## BASIC TRAINING PRINCIPLES: PUPPY VS. ADULT

There's a big difference between training an adult dog and training a young puppy. With a young puppy, everything is new! At 10 to 12 weeks of age, he will be experiencing many things, and he has nothing with which to compare these experiences. Up to this point, he has been with his dam and littermates, not one-on-one with people except in his interactions with his breeder and visitors to the litter.

When you first bring the puppy home, he is eager to please you. This means that he accepts doing things your way. During the next couple of months, he will absorb the basis of everything he needs to know for the rest of his life. This early age is even referred to as the "sponge" stage. After that, for the next 18 months, it's up to you to reinforce good manners by building on the foundation that you've established. Once your puppy is reliable in basic commands and behavior and has reached the appropriate age, you may gradually introduce him to some of the interesting sports, games and activities available to pet owners and their dogs.

Raising your puppy is a family affair. Each member of the family must know what rules to

### LEADER OF THE PACK

Canines are pack animals. They live according to pack rules, and every pack has only one leader. Guess what? That's you! To establish your position of authority, lay down the rules and be fair and good-natured in all your dealings with your dog. He will consider young children as his littermates, but the one who trains him, who feeds him, who grooms him, who expects him to come into line, that's his leader. And he who leads must be obeyed.

set forth for the puppy and how to use the same one-word commands to mean exactly the same thing every time. Even if yours is a large family, one person will soon be considered by the pup to be the leader, the Alpha person in his pack, the "boss" who must be obeyed. Often that highly regarded person turns out to be the one who feeds the puppy. Food ranks very high on the puppy's list of important things! That's why your puppy is rewarded with small treats along with verbal praise when he responds to you correctly. As the puppy learns to do what you want him to do, the food rewards are gradually eliminated and only the praise remains. If you were to keep up with the food treats, you could have two problems on your hands—an obese dog and a beggar.

Training begins the minute your Japanese Chin puppy steps through the doorway of your home, so don't make the mistake of putting the puppy on the floor and telling him by your actions to "Go for it! Run wild!" Even if this is your first puppy, you must act as if you know what you're doing: be the boss. An uncertain pup may be terrified to move, while a bold one will be ready to take you at your word and start plotting to destroy the house! Before you collected your puppy, you decided where his own special

Ready to absorb every lesson and good manner you can teach him, your Chin puppy is a living sponge for knowledge. Saturate him when he's young!

place would be, and that's where to put him when you first arrive home. Give him a house tour after he has investigated his area and had a nap and a bathroom "pit stop."

It's worth mentioning here that, if you've adopted an adult dog that is completely trained to your liking, lucky you! You're off the hook! However, if that dog spent his life up to this point in a kennel, or even in a good home but without any real training, be prepared to tackle the job ahead. A dog three years of age or older with no previous training cannot

---

**SHOULD WE ENROLL?**

If you have the means and the time, you should definitely take your dog to obedience classes. Begin with Puppy Kindergarten Classes in which puppies of all sizes learn basic lessons while getting the opportunity to meet and greet each other; it's as much about socialization as it is about good manners. What you learn in class, you can practice at home. And if you goof up in practice, you'll get help in the next session.

---

be blamed for not knowing what he was never taught. While the dog is trying to understand and learn your rules, at the same time he has to unlearn many of his previously self-taught habits and general view of the world.

Working with a professional trainer will speed up your progress with an adopted adult dog. You'll need patience, too. Some new rules may be close to impossible for the dog to accept. After all, he's been successful so far by doing everything his way! (Patience again.) He may agree with your instruction for a few

days and then slip back into his old ways, so you must be just as consistent and understanding in your teaching as you would be with a puppy. (More patience needed yet again!) Your dog has to learn to pay attention to your voice, your family, the daily routine, new smells, new sounds and, in some cases, even a new climate.

One of the most important things to find out about a newly adopted adult dog is his reaction to children (yours and others), strangers and your friends, and how he acts upon meeting other dogs. If he was not socialized with dogs as a puppy, this could be a major problem. This does not mean that he's a "bad" dog, a vicious dog or an aggressive dog; rather, it means that he has no idea how to read another dog's body language. There's no way for him to tell whether the other dog is a friend or foe. Survival instinct takes over, telling him to attack first and ask questions later. This definitely calls for professional help and, even then, may not be a behavior that can be corrected

It's no secret why treats are so helpful as training aids—just look at this Chin dance for joy when a tasty morsel is produced!

100% reliably (or even at all). If you have a puppy, this is why it is so very important to introduce your young puppy properly to other puppies and "dog-friendly" adult dogs.

## HOUSE-TRAINING YOUR JAPANESE CHIN

Dogs are tactility-oriented when it comes to house-training. In other words, they respond to the surface on which they are given approval to eliminate. The choice is yours (the dog's version is in parentheses): The lawn (including the neighbors' lawns)? A bare patch of earth under a tree (where people like to sit and relax in the summertime)? Concrete steps or patio (all sidewalks, garages and basement floors)? The curbside (watch out for cars)? A small area of crushed stone in a corner of the yard (mine!)? The latter is the best choice if you can manage it, because it will remain strictly for the dog's use and is easy to keep clean.

You can start out with paper-training indoors and switch over to an outdoor surface as the puppy

Some Chin are not born gardeners. Choose your Chin's relief area prudently, meaning an out-of-the-way place in the yard rather than the flowerbeds.

matures and gains control over his need to eliminate. For the nay-sayers, don't worry—this won't mean that the dog will soil on every piece of newspaper lying around the house. You are training him to go outside, remember? Starting out by paper-training often is the only choice for a city dog.

**WHEN YOUR PUPPY'S "GOT TO GO"**
Your puppy's need to relieve himself is seemingly non-stop, but signs of improvement will be seen each week. From 10–12 weeks old, the puppy will have to be taken outside every time he wakes up, about 10–15 minutes after

## LITTER BOXES
Small dogs that weigh up to about 20 pounds can be trained to use a litter box, though do not expect your cat to share his bathroom. For owners who are away from the house for more than four hours at a time, this is a real option. Small dogs can quickly learn to use the litter, almost as quickly as a cat learns. If you are unable to crate-train your small dog, the litter box provides a nice option to paper-training, although the dog will still need a safe place to stay when left alone.

every meal and after every period of play—all day long, from first thing in the morning until his bedtime! That's a total of ten or more trips per day to teach the puppy where it's okay to relieve himself. With that schedule in mind, you can see that house-training a young puppy is not a part-time job. It requires someone to be home all day.

If that seems overwhelming or impossible, do a little planning. For example, plan to pick up your puppy at the start of a vacation period. If you can't get home in the middle of the day, plan to hire a dog-sitter or ask a neighbor to come over to take the pup outside, feed him his lunch and then take him out again about ten or so minutes after he's eaten. Also make arrangements with that or

*Chin trained to their crates as puppies will accept their crates as places of refuge and privacy as adults.*

> **EXTRA! EXTRA!**
> The headlines read: "Puppy Piddles Here!" Breeders commonly use newspapers to line their whelping pens, so puppies learn to associate newspapers with relieving themselves. Do not use newspapers to line your pup's crate, as this will signal to your puppy that it is OK to urinate in his crate. If you choose to paper-train your puppy, you will layer newspapers on a section of the floor near the door he uses to go outside. You should encourage the puppy to use the papers to relieve himself, and bring him there whenever you see him getting ready to go. Little by little, you will reduce the size of the newspaper-covered area so that the puppy will learn to relieve himself "on the other side of the door."

another person to be your "emergency" contact if you have to stay late on the job. Remind yourself—repeatedly—that this hectic schedule improves as the puppy gets older.

### HOME WITHIN A HOME
Your Japanese Chin puppy needs to be confined to one secure, puppy-proof area when no one is able to watch his every move. Generally, the kitchen is the place of choice because the floor is washable. Likewise, it's a busy family area that will accustom the

# CANINE DEVELOPMENT SCHEDULE

It is important to understand how and at what age a puppy develops into adulthood. If you are a puppy owner, consult the following Canine Development Schedule to determine the stage of development your puppy is currently experiencing. This knowledge will help you as you work with the puppy in the weeks and months ahead.

| PERIOD | AGE | CHARACTERISTICS |
|---|---|---|
| FIRST TO THIRD | BIRTH TO SEVEN WEEKS | Puppy needs food, sleep and warmth and responds to simple and gentle touching. Needs mother for security and disciplining. Needs littermates for learning and interacting with other dogs. Pup learns to function within a pack and learns pack order of dominance. Begin socializing pup with adults and children for short periods. Pup begins to become aware of his environment. |
| FOURTH | EIGHT TO TWELVE WEEKS | Brain is fully developed. Pup needs socializing with outside world. Remove from mother and littermates. Needs to change from canine pack to human pack. Human dominance necessary. Fear period occurs between 8 and 12 weeks. Avoid fright and pain. |
| FIFTH | THIRTEEN TO SIXTEEN WEEKS | Training and formal obedience should begin. Less association with other dogs, more with people, places, situations. Period will pass easily if you remember this is pup's change-to-adolescence time. Be firm and fair. Flight instinct prominent. Permissiveness and over-disciplining can do permanent damage. Praise for good behavior. |
| JUVENILE | FOUR TO EIGHT MONTHS | Another fear period about 7 to 8 months of age. It passes quickly, but be cautious of fright and pain. Sexual maturity reached. Dominant traits established. Dog should understand sit, down, come and stay by now. |

NOTE: THESE ARE APPROXIMATE TIME FRAMES. ALLOW FOR INDIVIDUAL DIFFERENCES IN PUPPIES.

pup to a variety of noises, everything from pots and pans to the telephone, blender and dishwasher. He will also be enchanted by the smell of your cooking (and will never be critical when you burn something). An exercise pen (also called an "ex-pen," a puppy version of a playpen) within the room of choice is an excellent means of confinement for a young pup. He can see out and has a certain amount of space in which to run about, but he is safe from dangerous things like electrical cords, heating units, trash baskets

**A happy attitude on your part and plenty of positive reinforcement will travel down the leash to create a dog who loves to learn!**

## POTTY COMMAND

Most dogs love to please their masters; there are no bounds to what dogs will do to make their owners happy. The potty command is a good example of this theory. If toileting on command makes the master happy, then more power to him. Puppies will obligingly piddle if it really makes their keepers smile. Some owners can be creative about which word they will use to command their dogs to relieve themselves. Some popular choices are "Potty," "Tinkle," "Piddle," "Let's go," "Hurry up" and "Toilet." Give the command every time your puppy goes into position and the puppy will begin to associate his business with the command.

or open kitchen-supply cabinets. Place the pen where the puppy will not get a blast of heat or air conditioning.

In the pen, you can put a few toys, his bed (which can be his crate if the dimensions of pen and crate are compatible) and a few layers of newspaper in one small corner, just in case. A water bowl can be hung at a convenient height on the side of the ex-pen so it won't become a splashing pool for an innovative puppy. His food dish can go on the floor, next to the water bowl.

Crates are something that pet owners are at last getting used to for their dogs. Wild or domestic canines have always preferred to sleep in den-like safe spots, and that is exactly what the crate provides. How often have you seen adult dogs that choose to sleep under a table or chair even though they have full run of the house? It's the den connection.

In your "happy" voice, use the word "Crate" every time you put the pup into his den. If he's new to a crate, toss in a small biscuit for him to chase the first few times. At night, after he's been outside, he should sleep in his crate. The crate may be kept in his designated area at night or, if you want to be sure to hear those wake-up yips in the morning, put

The basic rule of house-training: what goes in must come out!

the crate in a corner of your bedroom. However, don't make any response whatsoever to whining or crying. If he's completely ignored, he'll settle down and get to sleep.

The size of the area or crate is the key factor here. The area must be large enough so that the puppy can lie down and stretch out, as well as stand up. At the same time, it must be small enough so that he cannot relieve himself at one end and sleep at the other without coming into contact with his droppings before he is fully trained to relieve himself outside. You can complicate toilet training by providing your Chin with a crate that is too spacious. You can use a removable divider panel to create a smaller space for the pup in the crate if needed during house-training.

Good bedding for a young

## DAILY SCHEDULE

How many relief trips does your puppy need per day? A puppy up to the age of 14 weeks will need to go outside about 8 to 12 times per day! You will have to take the pup out any time he starts sniffing around the floor or turning in small circles, as well as after naps, meals, games and lessons or whenever he's released from his crate. Once the puppy is 14 to 22 weeks of age, he will require only 6 to 8 relief trips. At the ages of 22 to 32 weeks, the puppy will require about 5 to 7 trips. Adult dogs typically require 4 relief trips per day, in the morning, afternoon, evening and late at night.

puppy is an old folded bath towel or an old blanket, something that is easily washable and disposable if necessary ("accidents" will happen!). Never put newspaper in the puppy's crate. Also, those old ideas about adding a clock to replace his mother's heartbeat, or a hot-water bottle to replace her warmth, are just that—old ideas. The clock could drive the puppy nuts, and the hot-water bottle could end up as a very soggy waterbed! An extremely good breeder would have introduced your puppy to the crate by letting two pups sleep together for a couple of nights, followed by several nights alone. How thankful you will be if you found that breeder!

Safe toys in the pup's crate or area will keep him occupied, but

*While it is important to provide your Chin with fresh water, you must monitor the amount of water he drinks during house-training. Do not leave a bowl of water in your dog's crate before he is fully house-trained or you will never succeed at toilet training.*

**I WILL FOLLOW YOU**
Obedience isn't just a classroom activity. In your home, you have many great opportunities to teach your dog polite manners. Allowing your pet on the bed or furniture elevates him to your level, which is not a good idea (the word is "Off!"). Use the "umbilical cord" method, keeping your dog on lead so he has to go with you wherever you go. You sit, he sits. You walk, he heels. You stop, he sit-stays. Everywhere you go, he's with you, but you go first!

monitor their condition closely. Discard any toys that show signs of being chewed to bits. Squeaky parts, bits of stuffing or plastic or any other small pieces can cause intestinal blockage or possibly choking if swallowed.

**PROGRESSING WITH POTTY-TRAINING**
After you've taken your puppy out and he has relieved himself in the area you've selected, he can have some free time with the family as long as there is someone responsible for watching him. That doesn't mean just someone in the same room who is watching TV or busy on the computer, but one person who is doing nothing other than keeping an eye on the pup, playing with him on the floor and helping him understand his position in the pack.

This first taste of freedom will

let you begin to set the house rules. If you don't want the dog on the furniture, now is the time to prevent his first attempts to jump up onto the couch. The word to use in this case is "Off," not "Down." "Down" is the word you will use to teach the down position, which is something entirely different.

Most corrections at this stage come in the form of simply distracting the puppy. Instead of telling him "No" for "Don't chew the carpet," distract the chomping puppy with a toy and he'll forget about the carpet.

As you are playing with the pup, do not forget to watch him closely and pay attention to his body language. Whenever you see him begin to circle or sniff, take the puppy outside to relieve himself. If you are paper-training, put him back into his confined area on the newspapers. In either case, praise him as he eliminates while he actually is in the act of relieving himself. Three seconds after he has finished is too late! You'll be praising him for running toward you, or picking up a toy or whatever he may be doing at that moment, and that's not what you want to be praising him for. Timing is a vital tool in all dog training. Use it!

Remove soiled newspapers immediately and replace them with clean ones. You may want to take a small piece of soiled paper

## LEASH TRAINING

House-training and leash training go hand in hand, literally. When taking your puppy outside to do his business, lead him there on his leash. Unless an emergency potty run is called for, do not whisk the puppy up into your arms and take him outside. If you have a fenced yard, you have the advantage of letting the puppy loose to go out, but it's better to put the dog on the leash and take him to his designated place in the yard until he is reliably house-trained. Taking the puppy for a walk is the best way to house-train a dog. The dog will associate the walk with his time to relieve himself, and the exercise of walking stimulates the dog's bowels and bladder. Dogs that are not trained to relieve themselves on a walk may hold it until they get back home, which of course defeats half the purpose of the walk.

and place it in the middle of the new clean papers, as the scent will attract him to that spot when it's time to go again. That scent attraction is why it's so important to clean up any messes made in the house by using a product specially made to eliminate the odor of dog urine and droppings. Regular household cleansers won't do the trick. Pet shops sell the best pet deodorizers. Invest in the largest container you can find!

Scent attraction eventually

## SOMEBODY TO BLAME

House-training a puppy can be frustrating for the puppy and the owner alike. The puppy does not instinctively understand the difference between defecating on the pavement outside and on the ceramic tile in the kitchen. He is confused and frightened by his human's exuberant reactions to his natural urges. The owner, arguably the more intelligent of the duo, is also frustrated that he cannot convince his puppy to obey his commands and instructions.

In frustration, the owner may struggle with the temptation to discipline the puppy, scold him or even strike him on the rear end. Physical corrections and harsh words are not only inappropriate but also will defeat your purpose in gaining your puppy's trust and respect. Don't blame your 12-week-old puppy. Blame yourself for not being 100% consistent in the puppy's lessons and routine. The lesson here is simple: try harder and your puppy will succeed.

will lead your pup to his chosen spot outdoors; this is the basis of outdoor training. When you take your puppy outside to relieve himself, use a one-word command such as "Outside" or "Go-potty" (that's one word to the puppy!) as you pick him up and attach his leash. Then put him down in his area. Now comes the hard part—hard for you, that is. Just stand there until he urinates and defecates. Move him a few feet in one direction or another if he's just sitting there looking at you, but remember that this is neither playtime nor time for a walk. This is strictly a business trip! Then, as he circles and squats (remember your timing!), give him a quiet "Good dog" as praise. If you start to jump for joy, ecstatic over his performance, he'll do one of two things: either he will stop mid-stream, as it were, or he'll do it again for you—in the house—and expect you to be just as delighted!

Give him five minutes or so and, if he doesn't go in that time, take him back indoors to his confined area and try again in another ten minutes, or immediately if you see him sniffing and circling. By careful observation, you'll soon work out a successful schedule.

Accidents, by the way, are just that—accidents. Clean them up quickly and thoroughly, without comment, after the puppy has been taken outside to finish his business and then put back into his area or crate. If you witness an accident in progress, say "No!" in a stern voice and get the pup outdoors immediately. No punishment is needed. You and your puppy are just learning each other's language, and sometimes it's easy to miss a puppy's message. Chalk it up to experience and watch more closely from now on.

## KEEPING THE PACK ORDERLY

Discipline is a form of training that brings order to life. For example, military discipline is what allows the soldiers in an army to work as one. Discipline is a form of teaching and, in dogs, is the basis of how the successful pack operates. Each member knows his place in the pack and all respect the leader, or Alpha dog. It is essential for your puppy that you establish this type of relationship, with you as the Alpha, or leader. It is a form of social coexistence that all canines recognize and accept. Discipline, therefore, is never to be confused with punishment. When you teach your puppy how you want him to behave, and he behaves properly and you praise him for it, you are disciplining him with a form of positive reinforcement.

For a dog, rewards come in the form of praise, a smile, a cheerful tone of voice, a few friendly pats or a rub of the ears.

**BE UPSTANDING!**
You are the dog's leader. During training, stand up straight so your dog looks up at you, and therefore up *to* you. Say the command words distinctly, in a clear, declarative tone of voice. (No barking!) Give rewards only as the correct response takes place (remember your timing!). Praise, smiles and treats are "rewards" used to positively reinforce correct responses. Don't repeat a mistake. Just change to another exercise—you will soon find success!

Rewards are also small food treats. Obviously, that does not mean bits of regular dog food. Instead, treats are very small bits of special things like cheese or pieces of soft dog treats. The idea is to reward the dog with something very small that he can taste and swallow, providing instant positive reinforcement. If he has to take time to chew a dry biscuit, he will have forgotten what he did to earn it by the time he is finished!

Your puppy should never be physically punished. The displeasure shown on your face and in your voice is sufficient to signal to the pup that he has done something wrong. He wants to please everyone higher up on the social ladder, especially his leader, so a scowl and harsh voice will take care of the error. Growling out the word "Shame!" when the pup is caught in the act of doing something wrong is better than the repetitive "No." Some dogs hear "No" so often that they begin to think it's their name! By the way, do not use the dog's

name when you're correcting him. His name is reserved to get his attention for something pleasant about to take place.

There are punishments that have nothing to do with you. For example, your dog may think that chasing cats is one reason for his existence. You can try to stop it as much as you like but without success, because it's such fun for the dog. But one good hissing, spitting, swipe of a cat's claws across the dog's nose will put an end to the game forever. Intervene only when your dog's eyeball is seriously at risk. Cat scratches can cause permanent damage to an innocent but annoying puppy.

## PUPPY KINDERGARTEN

### COLLAR AND LEASH
Before you begin your Japanese Chin puppy's education, he must be used to his collar and leash. Choose a collar for your puppy that is secure, but not heavy or bulky. He won't enjoy training if he's uncomfortable. A flat buckle collar is fine for everyday wear and for initial puppy training. For adult dogs, there are several types of training collars such as the martingale, which is a double loop that tightens slightly around the neck, or the head collar, which is similar to a horse's halter. Never use a chain choke collar with your Japanese Chin! A choke collar is much too harsh for

---

### BOOT CAMP
Even if one member of the family assumes the role of "drill sergeant," every other member of the family has to know what's involved in the dog's education. Success depends on consistency and knowing what words to use, how to use them, how to say them, when to say them and, most important to the dog, how to praise. The dog will be happy to respond to all members of the family, but don't make the little guy think he's in boot camp!

Your Chin will look to you for instruction and fairness. This delicate breed needs encouragement and equitable treatment in order to learn rules and commands.

*A little gentle pressure on your Chin's stubborn rear end will signal to him what is expected of him in the sit exercise.*

him to roam away from his area. The shorter leash will also be the one to use when you walk the puppy.

If you've been wise enough to enroll in a Puppy Kindergarten Training class, suggestions will be made as to the best collar and leash for your young puppy. I say "wise" because your puppy will be in a class with puppies in his age range (up to five months old) of all breeds and sizes. It's the perfect way for him to learn the right way (and the wrong way) to interact with other dogs as well as your tiny Toy, not to mention that it will pull and damage the Chin's long coat, so is doubly unsuitable for use on this breed.

A lightweight 6-foot woven cotton or nylon training leash is preferred by most trainers because it is easy to fold up in your hand and comfortable to hold because there is a certain amount of give to it. There are lessons where the dog will start off 6 feet away from you at the end of the leash. The leash used to take the puppy outside to relieve himself is shorter because you don't want

**DON'T STRESS ME OUT**

Your dog doesn't have to deal with paying the bills, the daily commute, PTA meetings and the like, but, believe it or not, there's a lot of stress in a dog's world. Stress can be caused by the owner's impatient demeanor and his angry or harsh corrections. If your dog cringes when you reach for his training collar, he's stressed. An older dog is sometimes stressed out when he goes to a new home. No matter what the cause, put off all training until he's over it. If he's going through a fear period—shying away from people, trembling when spoken to, avoiding eye contact or hiding under furniture—wait to resume training. Naturally you'd also postpone your lessons if the dog were sick, and the same goes for you. Show some compassion.

their people. You cannot teach your puppy how to interpret another dog's sign language. For a first-time puppy owner, these socialization classes are invaluable. For experienced dog owners, they are a real boon to further training.

### ATTENTION

You've been using the dog's name since the minute you collected him from the breeder, so you should be able to get his attention by saying his name—with a big smile and in an excited tone of voice. His response will be the puppy equivalent of "Here I am! What are we going to do?" Your immediate response (if you haven't guessed by now) is "Good dog." Rewarding him at the moment he pays attention to you teaches him the proper way to respond when he hears his name.

### EXERCISES FOR A BASIC CANINE EDUCATION

#### THE SIT EXERCISE

There are several ways to teach the puppy to sit. The first one is to catch him whenever he is about to sit and, as his backside nears the floor, say "Sit, good dog!" That's positive reinforcement and, if your timing is sharp, he will learn that what he's doing at that second is connected to your saying "Sit" and that you think he's clever for doing it!

Another method is to start with the puppy on his leash in front of you. Show him a treat in the palm of your right hand. Bring your hand up under his nose and, almost in slow motion, move your hand up and back so his nose goes up in the air and his head tilts back as he follows the treat in your hand. At that point, he will have to either sit or fall over, so as his back legs buckle under, say "Sit, good dog," and then give him the treat and lots of praise. You may have to begin with your hand lightly running up his chest, actually lifting his chin up until he sits. Some (usually older) dogs require very gentle pressure on their hindquarters with the left hand, in which case the dog should be on your left side. Puppies generally do not appreciate this physical dominance.

After a few times, you should be able to show the dog a treat in the open palm of your hand, raise your hand waist-high as you say "Sit" and have him sit. Once again, you have taught him two things at the same time. Both the verbal command and the motion of the hand are signals for the sit. Your puppy is watching you almost more than he is listening to you, so what you do is just as important as what you say.

Don't save any of these drills

*Once the down command is understood by your Chin, you can begin introducing hand signals into your exercises. A properly trained dog should respond to both voice and hand signals.*

only for training sessions. Use them as much as possible at odd times during a normal day. The dog should always sit before being given his food dish. He should sit to let you go through a doorway first, when the doorbell rings or when you stop to speak to someone on the street.

THE DOWN EXERCISE

Before beginning to teach the down command, you must consider how the dog feels about this exercise. To him, "Down" is a submissive position. Being flat on the floor with you standing over him is not his idea of fun. It's up to you to let him know that, while it may not be fun, the reward of your approval is worth his effort.

Start with the puppy on your left side in a sit position. Hold the leash right above his collar in

**TIME TO PLAY!**

Playtime can happen both indoors and out. A young puppy is growing so rapidly that he needs sleep more than he needs a lot of physical exercise. Puppies get sufficient exercise on their own just through normal puppy activity. Monitor play with young children so you can remove the puppy when he's had enough, or calm the kids if they get too rowdy. Almost all puppies love to chase after a toy you've thrown, and you can turn your games into educational activities. Every time your puppy brings the toy back to you, say "Give it" (or "Drop it") followed by "Good dog" and throwing it again. If he's reluctant to give it to you, offer a small treat so that he drops the toy as he takes the treat. He will soon get the idea.

issue the command sweetly, give him the treat and have the pup maintain the down position for several seconds. If he tries to get up immediately, place your hands on his shoulders and press down gently, giving him a very quiet "Good dog." As you progress with this lesson, increase the "down time" until he will hold it until you say "Okay" (his cue for release). Practice this one in the house at various times throughout the day.

By increasing the length of time during which the dog must maintain the down position, you'll find many uses for it. For example, he can lie at your feet in the vet's office or anywhere that both of you have to wait, when you are on the phone, while the family is eating and so forth. If you progress to training for competitive obedience, he'll

your left hand. Have an extra-special treat, such as a small piece of cooked chicken or hot dog, in your right hand. Place it at the end of the pup's nose and steadily move your hand down and forward along the ground. Hold the leash to prevent a sudden lunge for the food. As the puppy goes into the down position, say "Down" very gently.

The difficulty with this exercise is twofold: it's both the submissive aspect and the fact that most people say the word "Down" as if they were a drill sergeant in charge of recruits! So

Although the Chin is rather low to the ground, he likely will require a treat and gentle coaxing to fully assume the down position.

already be all set for the exercise called the "long down."

### THE STAY EXERCISE

You can teach your Japanese Chin to stay in the sit, down and stand positions. To teach the sit/stay, have the dog sit on your left side. Hold the leash at waist level in your left hand and let the dog know that you have a treat in your closed right hand. Step forward on your right foot as you say "Stay." Immediately turn and stand directly in front of the dog, keeping your right hand up high so he'll keep his eye on the treat hand and maintain the sit position for a count of five. Return to your original position and offer the reward.

Increase the length of the

*Your Chin will look to you for his next "assignment." Training reinforces the dog's desire to please you, both for tasty tidbits and jubilant praise.*

> **WHO'S TRAINING WHOM?**
> Dog training is a black-and-white exercise. The correct response to a command must be absolute, and the trainer must insist on completely accurate responses from the dog. A trainer cannot command his dog to sit and then settle for the dog's melting into the down position. Often owners are so pleased that their dogs "did something" in response to a command that they just shrug and say, "OK, Down" even though they wanted the dog to sit. You want your dog to respond to the command without hesitation; he must respond at that moment and correctly every time.

sit/stay each time until the dog can hold it for at least 30 seconds without moving. After about a week of success, move out on your right foot and take two steps before turning to face the dog. Give the "Stay" hand signal (left palm back toward the dog's head) as you leave. He gets the treat when you return and he holds the sit/stay. Increase the distance that you walk away from him before turning until you reach the length of your training leash. But don't rush it! Go back to the beginning if he moves before he should. No matter what the lesson, never be upset by having to back up for a few days. The repetition and practice are what will make your dog reliable in these commands. It won't do any good to move on to something more difficult if the command is not mastered at the easier levels. Above all, even if you do get frustrated, never let your puppy know! Always keep a positive, upbeat attitude during training, which will transmit to your dog for positive results.

The down/stay is taught in the same way once the dog is completely reliable and steady with the down command. Again, don't rush it. With the dog in the down position on your left side, step out on your right foot as you say "Stay." Return by walking around in back of the dog and into your original position. While you are training, it's okay to murmur something like "Hold on" to encourage him to stay put. When the dog will stay without moving when you are at a distance of 3 or 4 feet, begin to increase the length of time before you return. Be sure he holds the down on your return until you say "Okay." At that point, he gets his treat—just so he'll remember for next time that it's not over until it's over.

### THE COME EXERCISE

No command is more important to the safety of your Japanese Chin than "Come." It is what you should say every single time you see the puppy running toward

you: "Binky, come! Good dog." During playtime, run a few feet away from the puppy and turn and tell him to "Come" as he is already running to you. You can go so far as to teach your puppy two things at once if you squat down and hold out your arms. As the pup gets close to you and

*Teaching the sit/stay is the natural progression from the sit exercise. You can increase the time and distance of the stay with practice.*

### BASIC PRINCIPLES OF DOG TRAINING

1. Start training early. A young puppy is ready, willing and able.
2. Timing is your all-important tool. Praise at the exact time that the dog responds correctly. Pay close attention.
3. Patience is almost as important as timing!
4. Repeat! The same word has to mean the same thing every time.
5. In the beginning, praise all correct behavior verbally, along with treats and petting.

**NO MORE TREATS!**

When your dog is responding promptly and correctly to commands, it's time to eliminate treats. Begin by alternating a treat reward with a verbal-praise-only reward. Gradually eliminate all treats while increasing the frequency of praise. Overlook pleading eyes and expectant expressions, but if he's still watching your treat hand, you're on your way to using hand signals.

you're saying "Good dog," bring your right arm in about waist high. Now he's also learning the hand signal, an excellent device should you be on the phone when you need to get him to come to you! You'll also both be one step ahead when you enter obedience classes.

When the puppy responds to your well-timed "Come," try it with the puppy on the training leash. This time, catch him off guard, while he's sniffing a leaf or watching a bird: "Binky, come!" You may have to pause for a split second after his name to be sure you have his attention. If the puppy shows any sign of confusion, give the leash a mild jerk and take a couple of steps backward. Do not repeat the command. In this case, you should say "Good come" as he reaches you.

That's the number-one rule of

training. Each command word is given just once. Anything more is nagging. You'll also notice that all commands are one word only. Even when they are actually two words, you say them as one.

Never call the dog to come to you—with or without his name—if you are angry or intend to correct him for some misbehavior. When correcting the pup, you go to him. Your dog must always connect "Come" with something pleasant and with your approval; then you can rely on his response.

Puppies, like children, have notoriously short attention spans, so don't overdo it with any of the training. Keep each lesson short. Break it up with a quick run around the yard or a ball toss, repeat the lesson and quit as soon as the pup gets it right. That way, you will always end with a "Good dog."

Life isn't perfect and neither are puppies. A time will come, often around ten months of age, when he'll become "selectively deaf" or choose to "forget" his name. He may respond by wagging his tail (and even seeming to smile at you) with a look that says "Make me!" Laugh, throw his favorite toy and skip the lesson you had planned. Pups will be pups!

### THE HEEL EXERCISE
The second most important command to teach, after the come,

is the heel. When you are walking your growing puppy, you need to be in control. Besides, it looks terrible to be pulled and yanked down the street, and it's not much fun either. Your 10- to 12-week-old puppy will probably follow you everywhere, but that's his natural instinct, not your control over the situation. However, any time he does follow you, you can say "Heel" and be ahead of the game, as he will learn to associate this command with the action of following you before you even begin teaching him to heel.

There is a very precise, almost military, procedure for teaching your dog to heel. As with all other obedience training, begin with the dog on your left side. He will be in a very nice sit and you will have the training leash across your chest. Hold the loop and folded leash in your right hand. Pick up the slack leash above the dog in your left hand and hold it loosely at your side. Step out on your left foot as you say "Heel." If the puppy does not move, give a gentle tug or pat your left leg to get him started. If he surges ahead of you, stop and pull him back gently until he is at your side. Tell him to sit and begin again.

Walk a few steps and stop while the puppy is correctly beside you. Tell him to sit and give mild verbal praise. (More enthusiastic praise will encourage him to think the lesson is over.)

Repeat the lesson, increasing the number of steps you take only as long as the dog is heeling nicely beside you. When you end the lesson, have him hold the sit, then give him the "Okay" to let him know that this is the end of the lesson. Praise him so that he knows he did a good job.

### LET'S GO!

Many people use "Let's go" instead of "Heel" when teaching their dogs to behave on lead. It sounds more like fun! When beginning to teach the heel, whatever command you use, always step off on your left foot. That's the one next to the dog, who is on your left side, in case you've forgotten. Keep a loose leash. When the dog pulls ahead, stop, bring him back and begin again. Use treats to guide him around turns.

## OTHER ACTIVITIES

The Chin is a versatile little breed. Just because he's a Toy breed doesn't mean he can't compete in the same pursuits as the big dogs! Once he has basic obedience under his collar and is at least one year old, he can enter the world of agility training. Dogs think agility is pure fun, like being turned loose in an amusement park full of obstacles. Dogs compete against other dogs in their size category, with obstacles being reduced accordingly. In addition to agility, Chin have found success in obedience, tracking and other pursuits. As active little dogs, they enjoy backpacking with their owners (the rule of thumb is that no dog should carry more than one-sixth of his body weight). For those who like to volunteer, there is the wonderful feeling of owning a Therapy Dog and visiting hospices, nursing homes and veterans' homes to bring smiles, comfort and companionship to the residents. A breed club is a great source of information about the activities to which the Chin is well suited. At home, the kids in the family might enjoy teaching the Chin tricks, from playing hide-and-seek to dancing on his hind legs. A family dog is what rounds out the family! Everything he does, including gazing lovingly at you and curling up on your lap, represents the bonus of owning a dog.

The cure for excessive pulling (a common problem) is to stop when the dog is no more than 2 or 3 feet ahead of you. Guide him back into position and begin again. With a really determined puller, try switching to a head collar. This will automatically turn the pup's head toward you so you can bring him back easily to the heel position. Give quiet, reassuring praise every time the leash goes slack and he's staying with you.

Staying and heeling can take a lot out of a dog, so provide playtime and free-running exercise to shake off the stress when the lessons are over. You don't want him to associate training with all work and no fun.

### OBEDIENCE CLASSES

The advantages of an obedience class are that your dog will have to learn amid the distractions of other people and dogs and that your mistakes will be quickly corrected by the trainer. Teaching your dog along with a qualified instructor and other handlers who may have more dog experience than you is another plus of the class environment. The instructor and other handlers can help you to find the most efficient way of teaching your dog a command or exercise. It's often easier to learn by other people's mistakes than your own. You will also learn all of the requirements for competitive obedience trials, in which you can earn titles and go on to advanced exercises, which are fun for many dogs. The Japanese Chin has found success in obedience; his small size is no obstacle! Obedience classes build the foundation needed for many other canine activities (in which we humans are allowed to participate, too!).

# JAPANESE CHIN

## By Lowell Ackerman DVM, DACVD

## HEALTHCARE FOR A LIFETIME

When you own a dog, you become his healthcare advocate over his entire lifespan, as well as being the one to shoulder the financial burden of such care. Accordingly, it is worthwhile to focus on prevention rather than treatment, as you and your pet will both be happier.

Of course, the best place to have begun your program of preventive healthcare is with the initial purchase or adoption of your dog. There is no way of guaranteeing that your new furry friend is free of medical problems, but there are some things you can do to improve your odds. You certainly should have done adequate research into the Japanese Chin and have selected your puppy carefully rather than buying on impulse. Health issues aside, a large number of pet abandonment and relinquishment cases arise from a mismatch between pet needs and owner expectations. This is entirely preventable with appropriate planning and finding a good breeder.

Regarding healthcare issues specifically, it is very difficult to make blanket statements about where to acquire a problem-free pet, but, again, a reputable breeder is your best bet. In an ideal situation, you have the opportunity to see both parents, get

### TAKING YOUR DOG'S TEMPERATURE

It is important to know how to take your dog's temperature at times when you think he may be ill. It's not the most enjoyable task, but it can be done without too much difficulty. It's easier with a helper, preferably someone with whom the dog is friendly, so that one of you can hold the dog while the other inserts the thermometer.

Before inserting the thermometer, coat the end with petroleum jelly. Insert the thermometer slowly and gently into the dog's rectum about one inch. Wait for the reading, about two minutes. Be sure to remove the thermometer carefully and clean it thoroughly after each use.

A dog's normal body temperature is between 100.5 and 102.5 degrees F. Immediate veterinary attention is required if the dog's temperature is below 99 or above 104 degrees F.

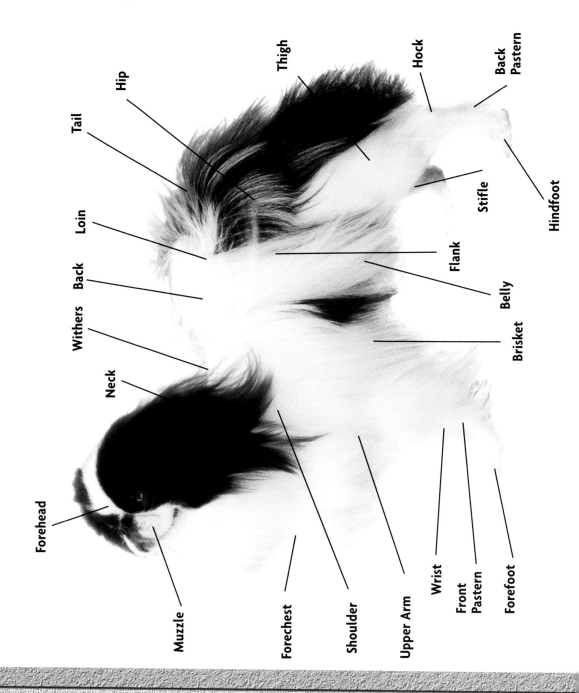

Thigh

Hip

Tail

Hock

Back
Pastern

Loin

Stifle

Hindfoot

Back

Flank

Withers

Belly

Neck

Brisket

Forehead

Muzzle

Forechest

Shoulder

Upper Arm

Wrist

Front
Pastern

Forefoot

# PHYSICAL STRUCTURE OF THE JAPANESE CHIN

references from other owners of the breeder's pups and see genetic-testing documentation for several generations of the litter's ancestors. At the very least, you must thoroughly investigate your breed of interest and the problems inherent in that breed, as well as the genetic testing available to screen for those problems. Genetic testing offers some important benefits, but testing is available for only a few disorders in a relatively small number of breeds and is not available for some of the most common genetic diseases, such as hip dysplasia, cataracts, epilepsy, cardiomy-opathy, etc. This area of research is indeed exciting and increasingly important, and advances will continue to be made each year. In fact, recent research has shown that there is an equivalent

dog gene for 75% of known human genes, so research done in either species is likely to benefit the other.

We've also discussed that evaluating the behavioral nature of your Japanese Chin and that of his immediate family members is an important part of the selection process that cannot be underestimated or underemphasized. It is sometimes difficult to evaluate temperament in puppies because certain behavioral tendencies, such as some forms of aggression, may not be immediately evident. More dogs are euthanized each year for behavioral reasons than for all medical conditions combined, so it is critical to take temperament issues seriously. Start with a well-balanced, friendly companion and put the time and effort into proper social-ization, and you will both be rewarded with a lifelong valued relationship.

Assuming that you have started off with a pup from healthy, sound stock, you then become responsible for helping your veterinarian keep your pet healthy. Some crucial things happen before you even bring your puppy home. Parasite control typically begins at two weeks of age, and vaccinations typically begin at six to eight weeks of age. A pre-pubertal evaluation is typically scheduled for about six months of age. At this time, a

## DOGGIE DENTAL DON'TS

A veterinary dental exam is necessary if you notice one or any combination of the following in your dog:
- Broken, loose or missing teeth
- Loss of appetite (which could be due to mouth pain or illness caused by infection)
- Gum abnormalities, including redness, swelling and bleeding
- Drooling, with or without blood
- Yellowing of the teeth or gumline, indicating tartar
- Bad breath

1. Esophagus
2. Lungs
3. Spleen
4. Liver
5. Stomach
6. Intestines
7. Urinary Bladder

# INTERNAL ORGANS OF THE JAPANESE CHIN

dental evaluation is done (since the adult teeth are now in), heartworm prevention is started and neutering or spaying is most commonly done.

It is critical to commence regular dental care at home if you have not already done so. It may not sound very important, but most dogs have active periodontal disease by four years of age if they don't have their teeth cleaned regularly at home, not just at their veterinary exams. Dental problems lead to more than just bad "doggie breath." Gum disease can have very serious medical consequences. If you start brushing your dog's teeth and using antiseptic rinses from a young age, your dog will be accustomed to it and will not resist. The results will be healthy dentition, which your Chin will need to enjoy a long, healthy life.

Most dogs are considered adults at around one year of age. Even individual dogs within each breed have different healthcare requirements, so work with your veterinarian to determine what will be needed and what your role should be. This doctor-client relationship is important, because as vaccination guidelines change, there may not be an annual "vaccine visit" scheduled. You must make sure that you see your veterinarian at least annually, even if no vaccines are due, because this is the best opportu-

## YOUR DOG NEEDS TO VISIT THE VET IF:

- He has ingested a toxin such as antifreeze or a toxic plant; in these cases, administer first aid and call the vet right away
- His teeth are discolored, loose or missing or he has sores or other signs of infection or abnormality in the mouth
- He has been vomiting, has had diarrhea or has been constipated for over 24 hours; call immediately if you notice blood
- He has refused food for over 24 hours
- His eating habits, water intake or toilet habits have noticeably changed; if you have noticed weight gain or weight loss
- He shows symptoms of bloat, which requires *immediate* attention
- He is salivating excessively
- He has a lump in his throat
- He has a lump or bumps anywhere on the body
- He is very lethargic
- He appears to be in pain or otherwise has trouble chewing or swallowing
- His skin loses elasticity

Of course, there will be other instances in which a visit to the vet is necessary; these are just some of the signs that could be indicative of serious problems that need to be caught as early as possible.

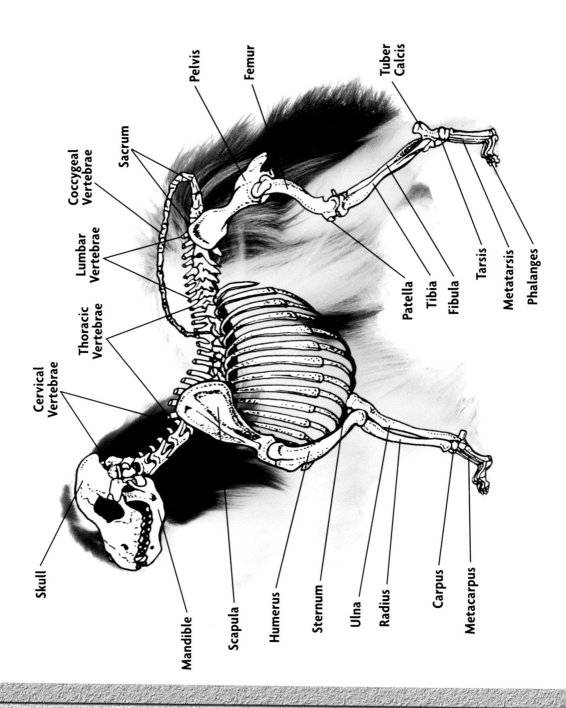

Pelvis

Femur

Tuber
Calcis

Sacrum

Coccygeal
Vertebrae

Lumbar
Vertebrae

Patella

Tibia

Fibula

Tarsis

Metatarsis

Phalanges

Thoracic
Vertebrae

Cervical
Vertebrae

Skull

Mandible

Scapula

Humerus

Sternum

Ulna

Radius

Carpus

Metacarpus

# SKELETAL STRUCTURE OF THE JAPANESE CHIN

nity to coordinate healthcare activities and to make sure that no medical issues creep by unaddressed.

**SELECTING A VETERINARIAN**
There is probably no more important decision that you will make regarding your pet's healthcare than the selection of his doctor. Your pet's veterinarian will be a pediatrician, family-practice physician and gerontologist, depending on the dog's life stage, and will be the individual who makes recommendations regarding issues such as when specialists need to be consulted, when diagnostic testing and/or therapeutic intervention is needed and when you will need to seek outside emergency and critical-care services. Your vet will act as your advocate and liaison throughout these processes.

Everyone has his own idea about what to look for in a vet, an individual who will play a big role in his dog's (and, of course, his own) life for many years to come. For some, it is the compassionate caregiver with whom they hope to develop a professional relationship to span the lifetime of their dogs and even their future pets. For others, they are seeking a clinician with keen diagnostic and therapeutic insight who can deliver state-of-the-art healthcare. Still others need a veterinary facility that is open evenings and weekends, or is in close proximity or provides mobile veterinary services, to accommodate their schedules; these people may not much mind that their dogs might see different veterinarians on each visit. Just as we have different reasons for selecting our own healthcare professionals (e.g., covered by insurance plan, expert in field, convenient location, etc.), we should not expect that there is a one-size-fits-all recommendation for selecting a veterinarian and veterinary practice. The best advice is to be honest in your assessment of what you expect from a veterinary practice and to conscientiously research the options in your area. You will quickly appreciate that not all veterinary practices are the same, and you will be happiest with one that truly meets the needs of you and your Japanese Chin.

There is another point to be considered in the selection of veterinary services. Not that long ago, a single veterinarian would attempt to manage all medical and surgical issues as they arose. That was often problematic, because veterinarians are trained in many species, breeds and diseases, and it was just impossible for general veterinary practitioners to be experts in every species, every field and every ailment. However, just as in the human healthcare fields, specialization has allowed general practitioners to concentrate

## PET INSURANCE

Pet-insurance policies are very cost-effective (and very inexpensive by human health-insurance standards), but make sure that you buy the policy long before you intend to use it (preferably starting in puppyhood, because coverage will exclude pre-existing conditions) and that you are actually buying an indemnity insurance plan from an insurance company that is regulated by your state or province. Many insurance policy look-alikes are actually discount clubs that are redeemable only at specific locations and for specific services. An indemnity plan covers your pet at almost all veterinary, specialty and emergency practices and is an excellent way to manage your pet's ongoing health-care needs.

on primary healthcare delivery, especially wellness and the prevention of infectious diseases, and to utilize a network of specialists to assist in the management of conditions that require specific expertise and experience. Thus there are now many types of veterinary specialists, including dermatologists, cardiologists, ophthalmologists, surgeons, internists, oncologists, neurologists, behaviorists, criticalists and others to help primary-care veterinarians deal with complicated medical challenges. In most cases,

specialists see cases referred by primary-care veterinarians, make diagnoses and set up management plans. From there, the animals' ongoing care is returned to their primary-care veterinarians. This important team approach to your pet's medical-care needs has provided opportunities for advanced care and an unparalleled level of quality to be delivered.

With all of the opportunities for your Japanese Chin to receive high-quality veterinary medical care, there is another topic that needs to be addressed at the same time—cost. It's been said that you can have excellent healthcare or inexpensive healthcare, but never both; this is as true in veterinary medicine as it is in human medicine. While veterinary costs are a fraction of what the same services cost in the human health-care arena, it is still difficult to deal with unanticipated medical costs, especially since they can easily creep into hundreds or even thousands of dollars if specialists or emergency services become involved. However, there are ways of managing these risks. The easiest is to buy pet health insurance and realize that its foremost purpose is not to cover routine healthcare visits but rather to serve as an umbrella for those rainy days when your pet needs medical care and you don't want to worry about whether or not you can afford that care.

## VACCINATIONS AND INFECTIOUS DISEASES

There has never been an easier time to prevent a variety of infectious diseases in your dog, but the advances we've made in veterinary medicine come with a price—choice. Now while it may seem that choice is a good thing (and it is), it has never been more difficult for the pet owner (or the veterinarian) to make an informed decision about the best way to protect pets through vaccination.

Years ago, it was just accepted that puppies got a starter series of vaccinations and then annual "boosters" throughout their lives to keep them protected. As more and more vaccines became available, consumers wanted the convenience of having all of that protection in a single injection. The result was "multivalent" vaccines that crammed a lot of protection into a single syringe. The manufacturers' recommendations were to give the vaccines annually, and this was a simple enough protocol to follow. However, as veterinary medicine has become more sophisticated and we have started looking more at healthcare quandaries rather than convenience, it became necessary to reevaluate the situation and deal with some tough questions. It is important to realize that whether or not to use a particular vaccine depends on the risk of contracting the disease against which it

protects, the severity of the disease if it is contracted, the duration of immunity provided by the vaccine, the safety of the product and the needs of the individual animal. In a very general sense, rabies, distemper, hepatitis and parvovirus are considered core vaccine needs, while parainfluenza, *Bordetella bronchiseptica*, leptospirosis, coronavirus and borreliosis (Lyme disease) are considered non-core needs and best reserved for animals that demonstrate reasonable risk of contracting the diseases.

## NEUTERING/SPAYING

Sterilization procedures (neutering for males/spaying for females) are meant to accomplish several purposes. While the underlying premise is to address the risk of pet overpopulation, there are also some medical and behavioral benefits to the surgeries as well. For females, spaying prior to the first estrus (heat cycle) leads to a marked reduction in the risk of mammary cancer. There also will be no manifestations of "heat" to attract male dogs and no bleeding in the house. For males, there is prevention of testicular cancer and a reduction in the risk of prostate problems. In both sexes, there may be some limited reduction in aggressive behaviors toward other dogs, and some diminishing of urine marking, roaming and mounting.

# COMMON INFECTIOUS DISEASES

Let's discuss some of the diseases that create the need for vaccination in the first place. Following are the major canine infectious diseases and a simple explanation of each.

**Rabies:** A devastating viral disease that can be fatal in dogs and people. In fact, vaccination of dogs and cats is an important public-health measure to create a resistant animal buffer population to protect people from contracting the disease. Vaccination schedules are determined on a government level and are not optional for pet owners; rabies vaccination is required by law in all 50 states.

**Parvovirus:** A severe, potentially life-threatening disease that is easily transmitted between dogs. There are four strains of the virus, but it is believed that there is significant "cross-protection" between strains that may be included in individual vaccines.

**Distemper:** A potentially severe and life-threatening disease with a relatively high risk of exposure, especially in certain regions. In very high-risk distemper environments, young pups may be vaccinated with human measles vaccine, a related virus that offers cross-protection when administered at four to ten weeks of age.

**Hepatitis:** Caused by canine adenovirus type 1 (CAV-1), but since vaccination with the causative virus has a higher rate of adverse effects, cross-protection is derived from the use of adenovirus type 2 (CAV-2), a cause of respiratory disease and one of the potential causes of canine cough. Vaccination with CAV-2 provides long-term immunity against hepatitis, but relatively less protection against respiratory infection.

**Canine cough:** Also called tracheobronchitis, actually a fairly complicated result of viral and bacterial offenders; therefore, even with vaccination, protection is incomplete. Wherever dogs congregate, canine cough will likely be spread among them. Intranasal vaccination with *Bordetella* and parainfluenza is the best safeguard, but the duration of immunity does not appear to be very long, typically a year at most. These are non-core vaccines, but vaccination is sometimes mandated by boarding kennels, obedience classes, dog shows and other places where dogs congregate to try to minimize spread of infection.

**Leptospirosis:** A potentially fatal disease that is more common in some geographic regions. It is capable of being spread to humans. The disease varies with the individual "serovar," or strain, of *Leptospira* involved. Since there does not appear to be much cross-protection between serovars, protection is only as good as the likelihood that the serovar in the vaccine is the same as the one in the pet's local environment. Problems with *Leptospira* vaccines are that protection does not last very long, side effects are not uncommon and a large percentage of dogs (perhaps 30%) may not respond to vaccination.

***Borrelia burgdorferi:*** The cause of Lyme disease, the risk of which varies with the geographic area in which the pet lives and travels. Lyme disease is spread by deer ticks in the eastern US and western black-legged ticks in the western part of the country, and the risk of exposure is high in some regions. Lameness, fever and inappetence are most commonly seen in affected dogs. The extent of protection from the vaccine has not been conclusively demonstrated.

**Coronavirus:** This disease has a high risk of exposure, especially in areas where dogs congregate, but it typically causes only mild to moderate digestive upset (diarrhea, vomiting, etc.). Vaccines are available, but the duration of protection is believed to be relatively short and the effectiveness of the vaccine in preventing infection is considered low.

There are many other vaccinations available, including those for *Giardia* and canine adenovirus-1. While there may be some specific indications for their use, and local risk factors to be considered, they are not widely recommended for most dogs.

While neutering and spaying do indeed prevent animals from contributing to pet overpopulation, even no-cost and low-cost neutering options have not eliminated the problem. Perhaps one of the main reasons for this is that individuals that intentionally breed their dogs and those that allow their animals to run at large are the main causes of unwanted offspring. Also, animals in shelters are often there because they were abandoned or relinquished, not because they came from unplanned matings. Neutering/spaying is important, but it should be considered in the context of the real causes of animals' ending up in shelters and eventually being euthanized.

One of the important considerations regarding neutering is that it is a surgical procedure. This sometimes gets lost in discussions of low-cost procedures and commoditization of the process. In females, spaying is specifically referred to as an ovario-hysterectomy. In this procedure, a midline incision is made in the abdomen and the entire uterus and both ovaries are surgically removed. While this is a major invasive surgical procedure, it usually has few complications, because it is typically performed on healthy young animals. However, it is major surgery, as any woman who has had a hysterectomy will attest.

In males, neutering has traditionally referred to castration, which involves the surgical removal of both testicles. While still a significant piece of surgery, there is not the abdominal exposure that is required in the female surgery. In addition, there is now a chemical sterilization option, in which a solution is injected into each testicle, leading to atrophy of the sperm-producing cells. This can typically be done under sedation rather than full anesthesia. This is a relatively new approach, and there are no long-term clinical studies yet available.

Neutering/spaying is typically done around six months of age at most veterinary hospitals, although techniques have been pioneered to perform the procedures in animals as young as eight weeks of age. In general, the surgeries on the very young animals are done for the specific reason of sterilizing them before they go to their new homes. This is done in some shelter hospitals for assurance that the animals will definitely not produce any pups. Otherwise, these organizations need to rely on owners to comply with their wishes to have the animals "altered" at a later date, something that does not always happen.

There are some exciting immunocontraceptive "vaccines" currently under development, and there may be a time when contraception in pets will not require surgical procedures. We anxiously await these developments.

A scanning electron micrograph of a dog flea, *Ctenocephalides canis*, on dog hair.

S. E. M. BY DR. DENNIS KUNKEL, UNIVERSITY OF HAWAII

## EXTERNAL PARASITES

### FLEAS

Fleas have been around for millions of years and, while we have better tools now for controlling them than at any time in the past, there still is little chance that they will end up on an endangered species list. Actually, they are very well adapted to living on our pets, and they continue to adapt as we make advances.

The female flea can consume 15 times her weight in blood during active reproduction and can lay as many as 40 eggs a day. These eggs are very resistant to the effects of insecticides. They hatch into larvae, which then mature and spin cocoons. The immature fleas reside in this pupal stage until the time is right for feeding. This pupal stage is also very resistant to the effects of insecticides, and pupae can last in the environment without feeding for many months. Newly emergent fleas are attracted to animals by the warmth of the animals' bodies, movement and exhaled carbon dioxide. However, when they first emerge from their cocoons, they orient towards light; thus when an animal passes between a flea and the light source, casting a shadow, the flea pounces and starts to feed. If the animal turns out to be a dog or cat, the reproductive cycle continues. If the flea lands on another type of animal, including a person, the flea will bite but will then look for a more appropriate host. An emerging adult flea can survive without feeding for up to 12 months but, once it tastes blood, it can survive off its host for only three to four days.

It was once thought that fleas spend most of their lives in the environment, but we now know that fleas won't willingly jump off a dog unless leaping to another dog or when physically removed by brushing, bathing or other manipulation. Flea eggs, on the other hand, are shiny and smooth, and they roll off the animal and into the environment. The eggs, larvae and pupae then exist in the environment, but once the adult finds a susceptible animal, it's home sweet home until the flea is forced to seek refuge elsewhere.

Since adult fleas live on the animal and immature forms survive in the environment, a successful treatment plan must address all stages of the flea life cycle. There are now several safe and effective flea-control products that can be applied on a monthly

> ## FLEA PREVENTION FOR YOUR DOG
> - Discuss with your veterinarian the safest product to protect your dog, likely in the form of a monthly tablet or a liquid preparation placed on the back of the dog's neck.
> - For dogs suffering from flea-bite dermatitis, a shampoo or topical insecticide treatment is required.
> - Your lawn and property should be sprayed with an insecticide designed to kill fleas and ticks that lurk outdoors.
> - Using a flea comb, check the dog's coat regularly for any signs of parasites.
> - Practice good housekeeping. Vacuum floors, carpets and furniture regularly, especially in the areas that the dog frequents, and wash the dog's bedding weekly.
> - Follow up house-cleaning with carpet shampoos and sprays to rid the house of fleas at all stages of development. Insect growth regulators are the safest option.

basis. These include fipronil, imidacloprid, selamectin and permethrin (found in several formulations). Most of these products have significant flea-killing rates within 24 hours. However, none of them will control the immature forms in the environment. To accomplish this, there are a variety of insect growth regulators that can be sprayed into

## THE FLEA'S LIFE CYCLE

What came first, the flea or the egg? This age-old mystery is more difficult to comprehend than the actual cycle of the flea. Fleas usually live only about four months. A female can lay 2,000 eggs in her lifetime.

**Egg**

After ten days of rolling around your carpet or under your furniture, the eggs hatch into larvae, which feed on various and sundry debris. In days or months, depending on the climate, the larvae spin cocoons and develop into the pupal or nymph stage, which quickly develop into fleas.

**Larva**

**Pupa**

These immature fleas must locate a host within 10 to 14 days or they will die. Only about 1% of the flea population exist as adult fleas, while the other 99% exist as eggs, larvae or pupae.

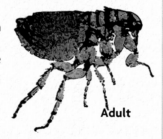

**Adult**

*Photo by Carolina Biological Supply Co.*

### KILL FLEAS THE NATURAL WAY

If you choose not to go the route of conventional medication, there are some natural ways to ward off fleas:
- Dust your dog with a natural flea powder, composed of such herbal goodies as rosemary, wormwood, pennyroyal, citronella, rue, tobacco powder and eucalyptus.
- Apply diatomaceous earth, the fossilized remains of single-cell algae, to your carpets, furniture and pet's bedding. Even though it's not good for dogs, it's even worse for fleas, which will dry up swiftly and die.
- Brush your dog frequently, give him adequate exercise and let him fast occasionally. All of these activities strengthen the dog's system and make him more resistant to disease and parasites.
- Bathe your dog with a capful of pennyroyal or eucalyptus oil.
- Feed a natural diet, free of additives and preservatives. Add some fresh garlic and brewer's yeast to the dog's morning portion, as these items have flea-repelling properties.

the environment (e.g., pyriprox-yfen, methoprene, fenoxycarb) as well as insect development inhibitors such as lufenuron that can be administered. These compounds have no effect on adult fleas, but they stop immature forms from developing into adults. In years gone by, we relied heavily on toxic insecti-cides (such as organophosphates, organochlorines and carbamates) to manage the flea problem, but today's options are not only much safer to use on our pets but also safer for the environment.

## TICKS

Ticks are members of the spider class (arachnids) and are blood-sucking parasites capable of transmitting a variety of diseases, including Lyme disease, ehrlichiosis, babesiosis and Rocky Mountain spotted fever. It's easy to see ticks on your own skin, but it is more of a challenge when your furry companion is affected. Whenever you happen to be planning a stroll in a tick-infested area (especially forests, grassy or wooded areas or parks) be prepared to do a thorough inspection of your dog afterward to search for ticks. Ticks can be tricky, so make sure you spend time looking in the ears, between the toes and everywhere else where a tick might hide. Ticks need to be attached for 24–72 hours before they transmit most of the diseases that they carry, so you do have a window of opportunity for some preventive intervention.

Female ticks live to eat and

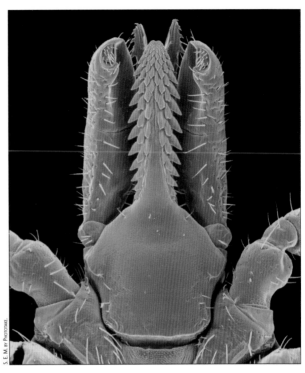

S. E. M. BY PHOTOTAKE.

**A TICKING BOMB**

There is nothing good about a tick's harpooning his nose into your dog's skin. Among the diseases caused by ticks are Rocky Mountain spotted fever, canine ehrlichiosis, canine babesiosis, canine hepatozoonosis and Lyme disease. If a dog is allergic to the saliva of a female wood tick, he can develop tick paralysis.

breed. They can lay between 4,000 and 5,000 eggs and they die soon after. Males, on the other hand, live only to mate with the females and continue the process as long as they are able. Most ticks live on multiple hosts before parasitizing dogs. The immature forms typically reside on grass and shrubs, waiting for susceptible animals to walk by. The larvae and nymph stages typically feed on wildlife.

If only a few ticks are present on a dog, they can be plucked out, but it is important to remove the entire head and mouthparts, which may be deeply embedded

A scanning electron micrograph of the head of a female deer tick, *Ixodes dammini*, a parasitic tick that carries Lyme disease.

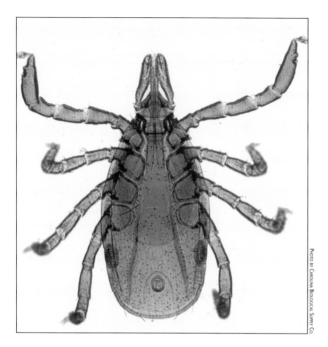

Photo by Carolina Biological Supply Co.

**Deer tick,** *Ixodes dammini.*

in the skin. This is best accomplished with forceps designed especially for this purpose; fingers can be used but should be protected with rubber gloves, plastic wrap or at least a paper towel. The tick should be grasped as closely as possible to the animal's skin and should be pulled upward with steady, even pressure. Do not squeeze, crush or puncture the body of the tick or you risk exposure to any disease carried by that tick. Once the ticks have been removed, the sites of attachment should be disinfected. Your hands should then be washed with soap and water to further minimize risk of contagion. The tick should be

disposed of in a container of alcohol or household bleach.

Some of the newer flea products, specifically those with fipronil, selamectin and permethrin, have effect against some, but not all, species of tick. Flea collars containing appropriate pesticides (e.g., propoxur, chlorfen-vinphos) can aid in tick control. In most areas, such collars should be placed on animals in March, at the beginning of the tick season, and changed regularly. Leaving the collar on when the pesticide level is waning invites the development of resistance. Amitraz collars are also good for tick control, and the active ingredient does not interfere with other flea-control products. The ingredient helps prevent the attachment of ticks to the skin and will cause those ticks already on the skin to detach themselves.

### TICK CONTROL
Removal of underbrush and leaf litter and the thinning of trees in areas where tick control is desired are recommended. These actions remove the cover and food sources for small animals that serve as hosts for ticks. With continued mowing of grasses in these areas, the probability of ticks' surviving is further reduced. A variety of insecticide ingredients (e.g., resmethrin, carbaryl, permethrin, chlorpyrifos, dioxathion and allethrin) are registered for tick control around the home.

## MITES

Mites are tiny arachnid parasites that parasitize the skin of dogs. Skin diseases caused by mites are referred to as "mange," and there are many different forms seen in dogs. These forms are very different from one another, each one warranting an individual description.

Sarcoptic mange, or scabies, is one of the itchiest conditions that affects dogs. The microscopic *Sarcoptes* mites burrow into the superficial layers of the skin and can drive dogs crazy with itchiness. They are also communicable to people, although they can't complete their reproductive cycle on people. In addition to being tiny, the mites also are often difficult to find when trying to make a diagnosis. Skin scrapings from multiple areas are examined microscopically but, even then, sometimes the mites cannot be found.

Fortunately, scabies is relatively easy to treat, and there are a variety of products that will successfully kill the mites. Since the mites can't live in the environment for very long without feeding, a complete cure is usually possible within four to eight weeks.

Cheyletiellosis is caused by a relatively large mite, which sometimes can be seen even without a microscope. Often referred to as "walking dandruff," this also causes itching, but not usually as profound as with scabies.

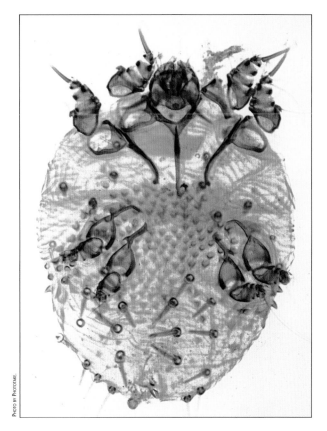

PHOTO BY PHOTOTAKE.

**Sarcoptes scabiei, commonly known as the "itch mite."**

While *Cheyletiella* mites can survive somewhat longer in the environment than scabies mites, they too are relatively easy to treat, being responsive to not only the medications used to treat scabies but also often to flea-control products.

*Otodectes cynotis* is the canine ear mite and is one of the more common causes of mange, especially in young dogs in shelters or pet stores. That's because the mites are typically present in large numbers and are quickly spread to

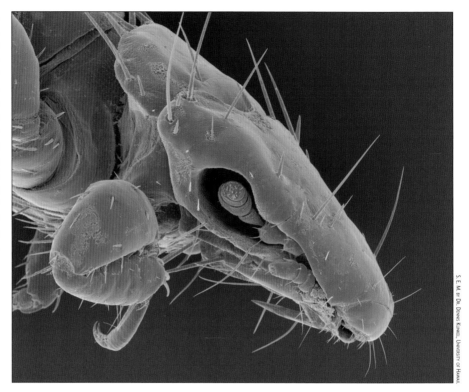

Micrograph of a dog louse, *Heterodoxus spiniger*. Female lice attach their eggs to the hairs of the dog. As the eggs hatch, the larval lice bite and feed on the blood. Lice can also feed on dead skin and hair. This feeding activity can cause hair loss and skin problems.

S. E. M. BY DR. DENNIS KUNKEL, UNIVERSITY OF HAWAII

nearby animals. The mites rarely do much harm but can be difficult to eradicate if the treatment regimen is not comprehensive. While many try to treat the condition with ear drops only, this is the most common cause of treatment failure. Ear drops cause the mites to simply move out of the ears and as far away as possible (usually to the base of the tail) until the insecticide levels in the ears drop to an acceptable level—then it's back to business as usual! The successful treatment of ear mites requires treating all animals in the household with a systemic insecticide, such as selamectin, or a combination of miticidal ear drops combined with whole-body flea-control preparations.

Demodicosis, sometimes referred to as red mange, can be one of the most difficult forms of mange to treat. Part of the problem has to do with the fact that the mites live in the hair follicles and they are relatively well shielded from topical and systemic products. The main issue, however, is that demodectic mange typically results only when there is some underlying process interfering with the dog's immune system.

Since *Demodex* mites are

normal residents of the skin of mammals, including humans, there is usually a mite population explosion only when the immune system fails to keep the number of mites in check. In young animals, the immune deficit may be transient or may reflect an actual inherited immune problem. In older animals, demodicosis is usually seen only when there is another disease hampering the immune system, such as diabetes, cancer, thyroid problems or the use of immune-suppressing drugs. Accordingly, treatment involves not only trying to kill the mange mites but also discerning what is interfering with immune function and correcting it if possible.

Chiggers represent several different species of mite that don't parasitize dogs specifically, but do latch on to passersby and can cause irritation. The problem is most prevalent in wooded areas in the late summer and fall. Treatment is not difficult, as the mites do not complete their life cycle on dogs and are susceptible to a variety of miticidal products.

### MOSQUITOES

Mosquitoes have long been known to transmit a variety of diseases to people, as well as just being biting pests during warm weather. They also pose a real risk to pets. Not only do they carry deadly heartworms but recently there also has been much concern over their involvement with West Nile virus. While we can avoid heartworm with the use of preventive medications, there are no such preventives for West Nile virus. The only method of prevention in endemic areas is active mosquito control. Fortunately, most dogs that have been exposed to the virus only developed flu-like symptoms and, to date, there have not been the large number of reported deaths in canines as seen in some other species.

Illustration of *Demodex folliculoram.*

ILLUSTRATION BY PHOTOTAKE

## MOSQUITO REPELLENT

Low concentrations of DEET (less than 10%), found in many human mosquito repellents, have been safely used in dogs but, in these concentrations, probably give only about two hours of protection. DEET may be safe in these small concentrations, but since it is not licensed for use on dogs, there is no research proving its safety for dogs. Products containing permethrin give the longest-lasting protection, perhaps two to four weeks. As DEET is not licensed for use on dogs, and both DEET and permethrin can be quite toxic to cats, appropriate care should be exercised. Other products, such as those containing oil of citronella, also have some mosquito-repellent activity, but typically have a relatively short duration of action.

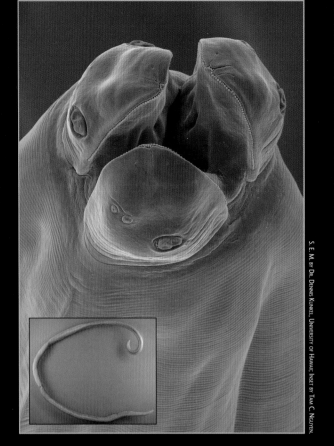

## ASCARID DANGERS

The most commonly encountered worms in dogs are roundworms known as ascarids. *Toxascaris leonine* and *Toxocara canis* are the two species that infect dogs. Subsisting in the dog's stomach and intestines, adult roundworms can grow to 7 inches in length and adult females can lay in excess of 200,000 eggs in a single day.

In humans, visceral larval migrans affects people who have ingested eggs of *Toxocara canis*, which frequently contaminates children's sandboxes, beaches and park grounds. The roundworms reside in the human's stomach and intestines, as they would in a dog's, but do not mature. Instead, they find their way to the liver, lungs and skin, or even to the heart or kidneys in severe cases. Deworming puppies is critical in preventing the infection in humans, and young children should never handle nursing pups who have not been dewormed.

The ascarid roundworm *Toxocara canis*, showing the mouth with three lips. INSET: Photomicrograph of the roundworm *Ascaris lumbricoides*.

## INTERNAL PARASITES: WORMS

### ASCARIDS

Ascarids are intestinal roundworms that rarely cause severe disease in dogs. Nonetheless, they are of major public health significance because they can be transferred to people. Sadly, it is children who are most commonly affected by the parasite, probably from inadvertently ingesting ascarid-contaminated soil. In fact, many yards and children's sandboxes contain appreciable numbers of ascarid eggs. So, while ascarids don't bite dogs or latch onto their intestines to suck blood, they do cause some nasty medical conditions in children and are best eradicated from our furry friends. Because pups can start passing ascarid eggs by three weeks of age, most parasite-control programs begin at two weeks of age and are repeated every two weeks until pups are eight weeks old. It is important to

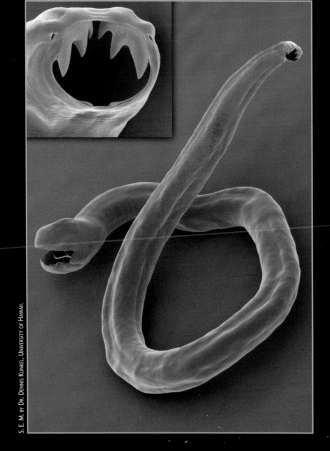

S. E. M. BY DR. DENNIS KUNKEL, UNIVERSITY OF HAWAII.

realize that bitches can pass ascarids to their pups even if they test negative prior to whelping. Accordingly, bitches are best treated at the same time as the pups.

### HOOKWORMS

Unlike ascarids, hookworms do latch onto a dog's intestinal tract and can cause significant loss of blood and protein. Similar to ascarids, hookworms can be transmitted to humans, where they cause a condition known as cutaneous larval migrans. Dogs can become infected either by consuming the infective larvae or by the larvae's penetrating the skin directly. People most often get infected when they are lying on the ground (such as on a beach) and the larvae penetrate the skin. Yes, the larvae can penetrate through a beach blanket. Hookworms are typically susceptible to the same medications used to treat ascarids.

The hookworm *Ancylostoma caninum* infests the intestines of dogs. INSET: Note the row of hooks at the posterior end, used to anchor the worm to the intestinal wall.

### WHIPWORMS

Whipworms latch onto the lower aspects of the dog's colon and can cause cramping and diarrhea. Eggs do not start to appear in the dog's feces until about three months after the dog was infected. This worm has a peculiar life cycle, which makes it more difficult to control than ascarids or hookworms. The good thing is that whipworms rarely are transferred to people.

Some of the medications used to treat ascarids and hookworms are also effective against whipworms, but, in general, a separate treatment protocol is needed. Since most of the medications are effective against the adults but not the eggs or larvae, treatment is typically repeated in three weeks, and then often in three

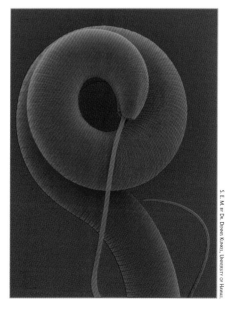

Adult whipworm, *Trichuris* sp., an intestinal parasite.

S. E. M. BY DR. DENNIS KUNKEL, UNIVERSITY OF HAWAII.

> **WORM-CONTROL GUIDELINES**
> • Practice sanitary habits with your dog and home.
> • Clean up after your dog and don't let him sniff or eat other dogs' droppings.
> • Control insects and fleas in the dog's environment. Fleas, lice, cockroaches, beetles, mice and rats can act as hosts for various worms.
> • Prevent dogs from eating uncooked meat, raw poultry and dead animals.
> • Keep dogs and children from playing in sand and soil.
> • Kennel dogs on cement or gravel; avoid dirt runs.
> • Administer heartworm preventives regularly.
> • Have your vet examine your dog's stools at your annual visits.
> • Select a boarding kennel carefully so as to avoid contamination from other dogs or an unsanitary environment.
> • Prevent dogs from roaming. Obey local leash laws.

months as well. Unfortunately, since dogs don't develop resistance to whipworms, it is difficult to prevent them from getting reinfected if they visit soil contaminated with whipworm eggs.

### TAPEWORMS

There are many different species of tapeworm that affect dogs, but *Dipylidium caninum* is probably the most common and is spread by fleas. Flea larvae feed on organic debris and tapeworm eggs in the environment and, when a dog chews at himself and manages to ingest fleas, he might get a dose of tapeworm at the same time. The tapeworm then develops further in the intestine of the dog.

The tapeworm itself, which is a parasitic flatworm that latches onto the intestinal wall, is composed of numerous segments. When the segments break off into the intestine (as proglottids), they may accumulate around the rectum, like grains of rice. While this tapeworm is disgusting in its behavior, it is not directly communicable to humans (although humans can also get infected by swallowing fleas).

A much more dangerous flatworm is *Echinococcus multilocularis*, which is typically found in foxes, coyotes and wolves. The eggs are passed in the feces and infect rodents, and, when dogs eat the rodents, the dogs can be infected by thousands of adult tapeworms. While the parasites don't cause many problems in dogs, this is considered the most lethal worm infection that people can get. Take appropriate precautions if you live in an area in which these tapeworms are found. Do not use mulch that may contain feces of

dogs, cats or wildlife, and discourage your pets from hunting wildlife. Treat these tapeworm infections aggressively in pets, because if humans get infected, approximately half die.

## HEARTWORMS

Heartworm disease is caused by the parasite *Dirofilaria immitis* and is seen in dogs around the world. A member of the roundworm group, it is spread between dogs by the bite of an infected mosquito. The mosquito injects infective larvae into the dog's skin with its bite, and these larvae develop under the skin for a period of time before making their way to the heart. There they develop into adults, which grow and create blockages of the heart, lungs and major blood vessels there. They also start producing

S. E. M. BY DR. DENNIS KUNKEL, UNIVERSITY OF HAWAII.

A dog tapeworm proglottid (body segment).

The dog tapeworm *Taenia pisiformis*.

S. E. M. BY DR. DENNIS KUNKEL, UNIVERSITY OF HAWAII.

## A Look at Internal Parasites

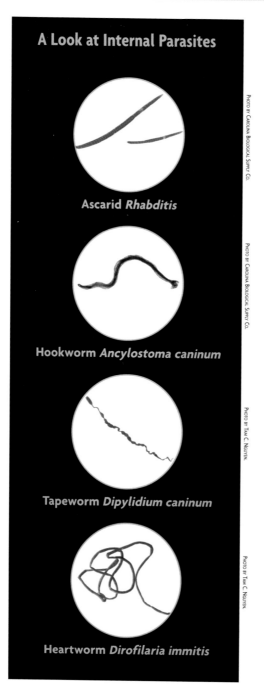

Ascarid *Rhabditis*

Hookworm *Ancylostoma caninum*

Tapeworm *Dipylidium caninum*

Heartworm *Dirofilaria immitis*

offspring (microfilariae) and these microfilariae circulate in the bloodstream, waiting to hitch a ride when the next mosquito bites. Once in the mosquito, the microfilariae develop into infective larvae and the entire process is repeated.

When dogs get infected with heartworm, over time they tend to develop symptoms associated with heart disease, such as coughing, exercise intolerance and potentially many other manifestations. Diagnosis is confirmed by either seeing the microfilariae themselves in blood samples or using immuno-logic tests (antigen testing) to identify the presence of adult heartworms. Since antigen tests measure the presence of adult heartworms and microfilarial tests measure offspring produced by adults, neither are positive until six to seven months after the initial infection. However, the beginning of damage can occur by fifth-stage larvae as early as three months after infection. Thus it is possible for dogs to be harboring problem-causing larvae for up to three months before either type of test would identify an infection.

The good news is that there are great protocols available for preventing heartworm in dogs. Testing is critical in the process, and it is important to understand the benefits as well as the limita-tions of such testing. All dogs six months of age or older that have not been on continuous heart-

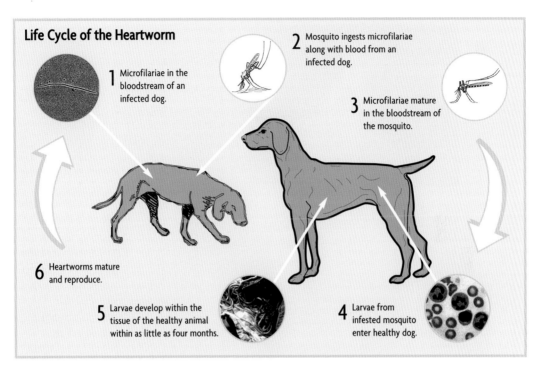

**Life Cycle of the Heartworm**

1 Microfilariae in the bloodstream of an infected dog.

2 Mosquito ingests microfilariae along with blood from an infected dog.

3 Microfilariae mature in the bloodstream of the mosquito.

4 Larvae from infested mosquito enter healthy dog.

5 Larvae develop within the tissue of the healthy animal within as little as four months.

6 Heartworms mature and reproduce.

worm-preventive medication should be screened with microfilarial or antigen tests. For dogs receiving preventive medication, periodic antigen testing helps assess the effectiveness of the preventives. The American Heartworm Society guidelines suggest that annual retesting may not be necessary when owners have absolutely provided continuous heartworm prevention. Retesting on a two- to three-year interval may be sufficient in these cases. However, your veterinarian will likely have specific guidelines under which heartworm preventives will be prescribed, and many prefer to err on the side of safety and retest annually.

It is indeed fortunate that heartworm is relatively easy to prevent, because treatments can be as life-threatening as the disease itself. Treatment requires a two-step process that kills the adult heartworms first and then the microfilariae. Prevention is obviously preferable; this involves a once-monthly oral or topical treatment. The most common oral preventives include ivermectin (not suitable for some breeds), moxidectin and milbemycin oxime; the once-a-month topical drug selamectin provides heartworm protection in addition to flea, tick and other parasite controls.

Breeders strive to produce Chin with clear, healthy eyes.

## A PET OWNER'S GUIDE TO COMMON OPHTHALMIC DISEASES
*by Prof. Dr. Robert L. Peiffer, Jr.*

Few would argue that vision is the most important of the cognitive senses, and maintenance of a normal visual system is important for an optimal quality of life. Likewise, pet owners tend to be acutely aware of their pets' eyes and vision, which is important because early detection of ocular disease will optimize therapeutic outcomes. The eye is a sensitive organ with minimal reparative capabilities, and with some diseases, such as glaucoma, uveitis and retinal detachment, early diagnosis and treatment can be critical in terms of whether vision can be preserved.

Lower entropion, or rolling in of the eyelid, is causing irritation in the left eye of this young dog. Several extra eyelashes, or distichiasis, are present on the lower lid.

The causes of ocular disease are quite varied; the nature of dogs make them susceptible to traumatic conditions, the most common of which include proptosis of the globe, cat scratch injuries and penetrating wounds from foreign objects, including sticks and air rifle pellets. Infectious diseases caused by bacteria, viruses or fungi may be localized to the eye or part of a systemic infection. Many of the common conditions, including eyelid conformational problems, cataracts, glaucoma and retinal degenerations, have a genetic basis.

Before acquiring your puppy, it is important to ascertain that both parents have been examined and certified free of eye disease by a veterinary ophthalmologist. Since many of these genetic diseases can be detected early in life, acquire the pup with the condition that he pass a thorough ophthalmic examination by a qualified specialist.

### LID CONFORMATIONAL ABNORMALITIES
Rolling in (entropion) or out (ectropion) of the lids tends to be specific to certain breeds. Entropion can involve the upper and/or lower lids. Signs usually appear between 3 and 12 months of age. The irritation

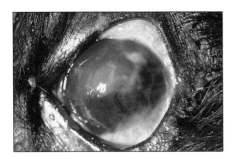

caused by the eyelid hairs' rubbing on the surface of the cornea may result in blinking, tearing and damage to the cornea. Ectropion is likewise breed-related and is considered "normal" in hounds, for instance; unlike entropion, which results in acute discomfort, ectropion may cause chronic irritation related to exposure and the pooling of secretions. Most of these cases can be managed medically with daily irrigation with sterile saline and topical antibiotics when required.

### EYELASH ABNORMALITIES

Dogs normally have lashes only on the upper lids, in contrast to humans. Occasionally, extra eyelashes may be seen emerging at the eyelid margin (distichiasis) or through the inner surface of the eyelid (ectopic cilia).

### CONJUNCTIVITIS

Inflammation of the conjunctiva, the pink tissue that lines the lids and the anterior portion of the sclera, is generally accompanied by redness, discharge and mild discomfort. The majority of cases are either associated with bacterial infections or dry eye syndrome. Fortunately, topical medications are generally effective in curing or controlling the problem.

### DRY EYE SYNDROME

Dry eye syndrome (keratoconjunctivitis sicca) is a common cause of external ocular disease. Discharge is typically thick and sticky, and keratitis is a frequent component; any breed can be affected. While some cases can be associated with toxic effects of drugs, including the sulfa antibiotics, the cause in the majority of the cases cannot be determined and is assumed to be immune-mediated.

Keratoconjunctivitis sicca, seen here in the right eye of a middle-aged dog, causes a characteristic thick mucous discharge as well as secondary corneal changes.

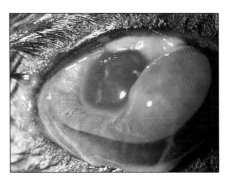

LEFT: Prolapse of the gland of the third eyelid in the right eye of a pup. RIGHT: In this case, in the right eye of a young dog, the prolapsed gland can be seen emerging between the edge of the third eyelid and the corneal surface.

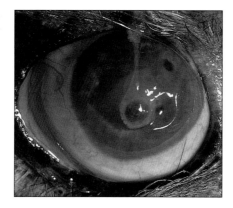

Multiple deep ulcerations affect the cornea of this middle-aged dog.

### PROLAPSE OF THE GLAND OF THE THIRD EYELID

In this condition, commonly referred to as *cherry eye*, the gland of the third eyelid, which produces about one-third of the aqueous phase of the tear film and is normally situated within the anterior orbit, prolapses to emerge as a pink fleshy mass protruding over the edge of the third eyelid, between the third eyelid and the cornea. The condition usually develops during the first year of life and, while mild irritation may result, the condition is unsightly as much as anything else.

Lipid deposition can occur as a primary inherited dystrophy, or secondarily to hypercholesterolemia (in dogs frequently associated with hypothyroidism), chronic corneal inflammation or neoplasia. The deposits in this dog assume an oval pattern in the center of the cornea.

### CORNEAL DISEASE

The cornea is the clear front part of the eye that provides the first step in the collection of light on its journey to be eventually focused onto the retina, and most corneal diseases will be manifested by alterations in corneal transparency. The cornea is an exquisitely innervated tissue, and defects in corneal integrity are accompanied by pain, which is demonstrated by squinting.

Corneal ulcers may occur secondarily to trauma or to irritation from entropion or ectopic cilia. In middle-aged or older dogs, epithelial ulcerations may occur spontaneously due to an inherent defect; these are referred to as indolent or Boxer ulcers, in recognition of the breed in which we see the condition most frequently. Infection may occur secondarily. Ulcers can be potentially blinding conditions; severity is dependent upon the size and depth of the ulcer and other complicating features.

Non-ulcerative keratitis tends to have an immune-mediated component and is managed by topical immunosuppressants, usually corticosteroids. Corneal edema can occur in elderly dogs. It is due to a failure of the corneal endothelial "pump."

The cornea responds to chronic irritation by transforming

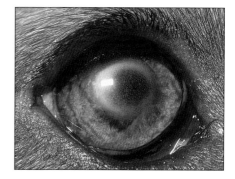

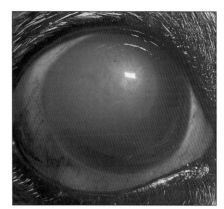

into skin-like tissue that is evident clinically by pigmentation, scarring and vascularization; some cases may respond to tear stimulants, lubricants and topical corticosteroids, while others benefit from surgical narrowing of the eyelid opening in order to enhance corneal protection.

## UVEITIS

Inflammation of the vascular tissue of the eye—the uvea—is a common and potentially serious disease in dogs. While it may occur secondarily to trauma or other intraocular diseases, such as cataracts, most commonly uveitis is associated with some type of systemic infectious or neoplastic process. Uncontrolled, uveitis can lead to blinding cataracts, glaucoma and/or retinal detachments, and aggressive symptomatic therapy with dilating agents (to prevent pupillary adhesions) and anti-inflammatories are critical.

## GLAUCOMA

The eye is essentially a hollow fluid-filled sphere, and the pressure within is maintained by regulation of the rate of fluid production and fluid egress at 10–20 mms of mercury. The retinal cells are extremely sensitive to elevations of intraocular pressure and, unless controlled, permanent blindness can occur within hours to days. In acute glaucoma, the conjunctiva becomes congested, the cornea cloudy, the pupil moderate and fixed; the eye is generally painful and avisual. Increased constant signs of

Corneal edema can develop as a slowly progressive process in elderly Boston Terriers, Miniature Dachshunds and Miniature Poodles, as well as others, as a result of the inability of the corneal endothelial "pump" to maintain a state of dehydration.

Medial pigmentary keratitis in this dog is associated with irritation from prominent facial folds.

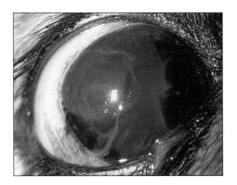

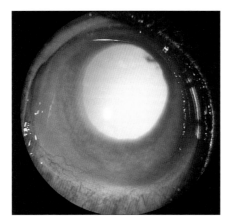

Glaucoma in the dog most commonly occurs as a sudden extreme elevation of intraocular pressure, frequently to three to four times the norm. The eye of this dog demonstrates the common signs of episcleral injection, or redness; mild diffuse corneal cloudiness, due to edema; and a mid-sized fixed pupil.

discomfort will accompany chronic cases.

Management of glaucoma is one of the most challenging situations the veterinary ophthalmologist faces; in spite of intense efforts, many of these cases will result in blindness.

**CATARACTS AND LENS DISLOCATION**
Cataracts are the most common blinding condition in dogs and the main eye problem seen in the Chin; fortunately, they are readily amenable to surgical intervention, with excellent results in terms of

restoration of vision and replacement of the cataractous lens with a synthetic one. Most cataracts in dogs are inherited; less commonly cataracts can be secondary to trauma or other ocular diseases, including uveitis, glaucoma, lens luxation and retinal degeneration, or secondary to an underlying systemic metabolic disease, including diabetes and Cushing's disease. Signs include a progressive loss of the bright dark appearance of the pupil, which is replaced by a blue-gray hazy appearance. In this respect, cataracts need to be distinguished from the normal aging process of nuclear sclerosis, which occurs in middle-aged or older animals, and has minimal effect on vision.

Lens dislocation occurs in dogs and frequently leads to secondary glaucoma; early removal of the dislocated lens is generally curative.

**RETINAL DISEASE**
Retinal degenerations are usually inherited, but may be associated

LEFT: The typical posterior subcapsular cataract appears between one and two years of age, but rarely progresses to where the animal has visual problems. RIGHT: Inherited cataracts generally appear between three and six years of age, and progress to the stage seen where functional vision is significantly impaired.

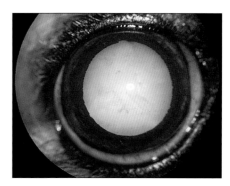

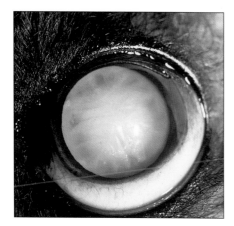

with vitamin E deficiency in dogs. While signs are variable, most frequently one notes a decrease in vision over a period of months, which typically starts out as night blindness. The cause of a more rapid loss of vision due to retinal degeneration occurs over days to weeks is labeled sudden acquired retinal degeneration or SARD; the outcome, however, is unfortunately usually similar to inherited and nutritional conditions, as the

retinal tissues possess minimal regenerative capabilities. Most pets, however, with a bit of extra care and attention, show an amazing ability to adapt to an avisual world, and can be maintained as pets with a satisfactory quality of life.

Detachment of the retina—due to accumulation of blood between the retina and the underling uvea, which is called the *choroid*—can occur secondarily to retinal tears or holes, tractional forces within the eye, or as a result of uveitis. These types of detachments may be amenable to surgical repair if diagnosed early.

### OPTIC NERVE

Optic neuritis, or inflammation of the nerve that connects the eye with the brain stem, is a relatively uncommon condition that presents usually with rather sudden loss of vision and widely dilated non-responsive pupils.

Anterior lens luxation can occur as a primary disease in the terrier breeds, or secondarily to trauma. The fibers that hold the lens in place rupture and the lens may migrate through the pupil to be situated in front of the iris. Secondary glaucoma is a frequent and significant complication that can be avoided if the dislocated lens is removed surgically.

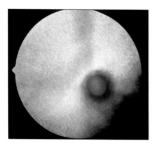
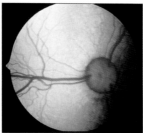
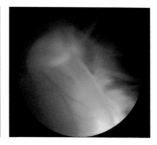
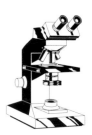

**LEFT:** The posterior pole of a normal fundus is shown; prominent are the head of the optic nerve and the retinal blood vessels. The retina is transparent, and the prominent green tapetum is seen superiorly.
**CENTER:** An eye with inherited retinal dysplasia is depicted. The tapetal retina superior to the optic disc is disorganized, with multifocal areas of hyperplasia of the retinal pigment epithelium.
**RIGHT:** Severe collie eye anomaly and a retinal detachment; this eye is unfortunately blind.

# THE **ABC**s OF
# Emergency Care

## Abrasions
Clean wound with running water or 3% hydrogen peroxide. Pat dry with gauze and spray with antibiotic. Do not cover.

## Animal Bites
Clean area with soap and saline solution or water. Apply pressure to any bleeding area. Apply antibiotic ointment.

## Antifreeze Poisoning
Induce vomiting and take dog to the vet.

## Bee Sting
Remove stinger and apply soothing lotion or cold compress; give antihistamine in proper dosage.

## Bleeding
Apply pressure directly to wound with gauze or towel for five to ten minutes. If wound does not stop bleeding, wrap wound with gauze and adhesive tape.

## Bloat/Gastric Torsion
Immediately take the dog to the vet or emergency clinic; phone from car. No time to waste.

## Burns
**Chemical:** Bathe dog with water and pet shampoo. Rinse in saline solution. Apply antibiotic ointment.

**Acid:** Rinse with water. Apply one part baking soda, two parts water to affected area.

**Alkali:** Rinse with water. Apply one part vinegar, four parts water to affected area.

**Electrical:** Apply antibiotic ointment. Seek veterinary assistance immediately.

## Choking
If the dog is on the verge of collapsing, wedge a solid object, such as the handle of screwdriver, between molars on one side of the mouth to keep mouth open. Pull tongue out. Use long-nosed pliers or fingers to remove foreign object. Do not push the object down the dog's throat. For small or medium dogs, hold dog upside down by hind legs and shake firmly to dislodge foreign object.

## Chlorine Ingestion
With clean water, rinse the mouth and eyes. Give the dog water to drink; contact the vet.

## Constipation
Feed dog 2 tablespoons bran flakes with each meal. Encourage drinking water. Mix 1/4 teaspoon mineral oil in dog's food.

## Diarrhea
Withhold food for 12 to 24 hours. Feed dog antidiarrheal with eyedropper. When feeding resumes, feed one part boiled hamburger, one part plain cooked rice, 1/4 to 3/4 cup four times daily.

## Dog Bite
Snip away hair around puncture wound; clean with 3% hydrogen peroxide; apply tincture of iodine. If wound appears deep, take the dog to the vet.

## Frostbite
Wrap the dog in a heavy blanket. Warm affected area with a warm bath for ten minutes. Red color to skin will return with circulation; if tissues are pale after 20 minutes, contact the vet.

*Use a portable, durable container large enough to contain all items*

## DOG OWNER'S FIRST-AID KIT

- ❑ **Gauze bandages/swabs**
- ❑ **Adhesive and non-adhesive bandages**
- ❑ **Antibiotic powder**
- ❑ **Antiseptic wash**
- ❑ **Hydrogen peroxide 3%**
- ❑ **Antibiotic ointment**
- ❑ **Lubricating jelly**
- ❑ **Rectal thermometer**
- ❑ **Nylon muzzle**
- ❑ **Scissors and forceps**
- ❑ **Eyedropper**
- ❑ **Syringe**
- ❑ **Anti-bacterial/fungal solution**
- ❑ **Saline solution**
- ❑ **Antihistamine**
- ❑ **Cotton balls**
- ❑ **Nail clippers**
- ❑ **Screwdriver/pen knife**
- ❑ **Flashlight**
- ❑ **Emergency phone numbers**

### Heat Stroke
Partially submerge the dog in cold water; if no response within ten minutes, contact the vet.

### Hot Spots
Mix 2 packets Domeboro® with 2 cups water. Saturate cloth with mixture and apply to hot spots for 15 to 30 minutes. Apply antibiotic ointment. Repeat every six to eight hours.

### Poisonous Plants
Wash affected area with soap and water. Cleanse with alcohol. For foxtail/grass, apply antibiotic ointment.

### Rat Poison Ingestion
Induce vomiting. Keep dog calm, maintain dog's normal body temperature (use blanket or heating pad). Get to the vet for antidote.

### Shock
Keep the dog calm and warm; call for veterinary assistance.

### Snake Bite
If possible, bandage the area and apply pressure. If the area is not conducive to bandaging, use ice to control bleeding. Get immediate help from the vet.

### Tick Removal
Apply flea and tick spray directly on tick. Wait one minute. Using tweezers or wearing plastic gloves, apply constant pressure while grasping tick's body and pull out. Apply antibiotic ointment.

### Vomiting
Restrict dog's water intake; offer a few ice cubes. Withhold food for next meal. Contact vet if vomiting persists longer than 24 hours.

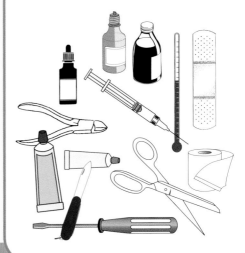

# Number-One Killer Disease in Dogs: CANCER

In every age, there is a word associated with a disease or plague that causes humans to shudder. In the 21st century, that word is "cancer." Just as cancer is the leading cause of death in humans, it claims nearly half the lives of dogs that die from a natural disease as well as half the dogs that die over the age of ten years.

Described as a genetic disease, cancer becomes a greater risk as the dog ages. Vets and dog owners have become increasingly aware of the threat of cancer to dogs. Statistics reveal that one dog in every five will develop cancer, the most common of which is skin cancer. Many cancers, including prostate, ovarian and breast cancer, can be avoided by spaying and neutering our dogs by the age of six months.

Early detection of cancer can save or extend a dog's life, so it is absolutely vital for owners to have their dogs examined by a qualified vet or oncologist immediately upon detection of any abnormality. Certain dietary guidelines have also proven to reduce the onset and spread of cancer. Foods based on fish rather than beef, due to the presence of Omega-3 fatty acids, are recommended. Other amino acids such as glutamine have significant benefits for canines, particularly those breeds that show a greater susceptibility to cancer.

Cancer management and treatments promise hope for future generations of canines. Since the disease is genetic, breeders should never breed a dog whose parents, grandparents and any related siblings have developed cancer. It is difficult to know whether to exclude an otherwise healthy dog from a breeding program, as the disease does not manifest itself until the dog's senior years.

## RECOGNIZE CANCER WARNING SIGNS

Since early detection can possibly rescue your dog from becoming a cancer statistic, it is essential for owners to recognize the possible signs and seek the assistance of a qualified professional.

- Abnormal bumps or lumps that continue to grow
- Bleeding or discharge from any body cavity
- Persistent stiffness or lameness
- Recurrent sores or sores that do not heal
- Inappetence
- Breathing difficulties
- Weight loss
- Bad breath or odors
- General malaise and fatigue
- Eating and swallowing problems
- Difficulty urinating and defecating

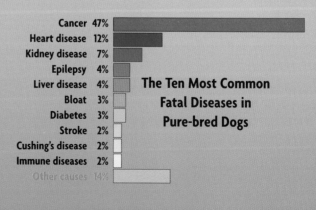

| | |
|---|---|
| Cancer | 47% |
| Heart disease | 12% |
| Kidney disease | 7% |
| Epilepsy | 4% |
| Liver disease | 4% |
| Bloat | 3% |
| Diabetes | 3% |
| Stroke | 2% |
| Cushing's disease | 2% |
| Immune diseases | 2% |
| Other causes | 14% |

**The Ten Most Common Fatal Diseases in Pure-bred Dogs**

# CANINE COGNITIVE DYSFUNCTION

## "OLD-DOG" SYNDROME

There are many ways for you to evaluate old-dog syndrome. Veterinarians have defined canine cognitive dysfunction as the gradual deterioration of cognitive abilities, indicated by changes in the dog's behavior. When a dog changes his routine response, and maladies have been eliminated as the cause of these behavioral changes, then canine cognitive dysfunction is the usual diagnosis.

More than half the dogs over eight years old suffer from some form of this syndrome. The older the dog, the more chance he has of suffering from it. In humans, doctors often dismiss the canine cognitive dysfunction behavioral changes as part of "winding down."

There are four major signs of canine cognitive dysfunction: frequent potty accidents inside the home, sleeping much more or much less than normal, acting confused and failing to respond to social stimuli.

## SYMPTOMS

### FREQUENT POTTY ACCIDENTS
- Urinates in the house.
- Defecates in the house.
- Doesn't signal that he wants to go out.

### FAILURE TO RESPOND TO SOCIAL STIMULI
- Comes to people less frequently, whether called or not.
- Doesn't tolerate petting for more than a short time.
- Doesn't come to the door when you return home.

### CONFUSION
- Goes outside and just stands there.
- Appears confused with a faraway look in his eyes.
- Hides more often.
- Doesn't recognize friends.
- Doesn't come when called.
- Walks around listlessly and without a destination.

### SLEEP PATTERNS
- Awakens more slowly.
- Sleeps more than normal during the day.
- Sleeps less during the night.

When we bring home a puppy, full of the energy and exuberance that accompanies youth, we hope for a long, happy and fulfilling relationship with the new family member. Even when we adopt an older dog, we look forward to the years of companionship ahead with a new canine friend. However, aging is inevitable for all creatures, and there will come a time when your Japanese Chin reaches his senior years and will need special considerations and attention to his care.

### WHEN IS MY DOG A "SENIOR"?

In general, pure-bred dogs are considered to have achieved senior status when they reach 75% of their breed's average lifespan, with lifespan being based generally on breed size along with breed-specific factors. Your Chin has an average lifespan of 10–12 years, although dogs that remain healthy can certainly live longer. The Chin is considered a senior at around seven to eight years old.

Obviously, the old "seven dog years to one human year" theory is not exact. In puppyhood, a dog's year is actually comparable to more than seven human years, considering the puppy's rapid growth during his first year. Then, in adulthood, the ratio decreases. Regardless, the more viable rule of thumb is that the larger the dog, the shorter his expected lifespan. Of course, this can vary among individual dogs, with many living longer than expected, which we hope is the case!

### WHAT ARE THE SIGNS OF AGING?

By the time your dog has reached his senior years, you will know him very well, so the physical and behavioral changes that accompany aging should be noticeable to you. Humans and dogs share the most obvious physical sign of aging: gray hair! Graying often occurs first on the muzzle and face, around the eyes. Other telltale signs are the dog's overall decrease in activity. Your older dog might be more content to nap and rest, and he may not show the same old enthusiasm when it's time to play in the yard or go for a walk. Other physical signs include significant weight loss or gain; more labored movement; skin and coat problems, possibly hair loss; sight and/or hearing problems; changes

Although the elderly Japanese Chin does not approach life with the same vigor that a young dog does, he is still a loving companion who enjoys life's simple pleasures.

in toileting habits, perhaps seeming "unhousebroken" at times; and tooth decay, bad breath or other mouth problems.

There are behavioral changes that go along with aging, too. There are numerous causes for behavioral changes. Sometimes a dog's apparent confusion results from a physical change like diminished sight or hearing. If his confusion causes him to be afraid, he may act aggressively or defensively. He may sleep more frequently because his daily walks, though shorter now, tire him out. He may begin to experience separation anxiety or, conversely, become less interested in petting and attention.

There also are clinical conditions that cause behavioral changes in older dogs. One such condition is known as canine cognitive dysfunction (familiarly known as "old-dog" syndrome). It can be frustrating for an owner whose dog is affected with cognitive dysfunction, as it can result in behavioral changes of all types, most seemingly unexplainable. Common changes include the dog's forgetting aspects of the daily routine, such as times to eat, go out for walks, relieve himself and the like. Along the same lines, you may take your dog out at the regular time for a potty trip and he may have no idea why he is there. Sometimes a placid dog will begin to show aggressive or possessive

tendencies or, conversely, a hyperactive dog will start to "mellow out."

Disease also can be the cause of behavioral changes in senior dogs. Hormonal problems (Cushing's disease is common in older dogs), diabetes and thyroid disease can cause increased appetite, which can lead to aggression related to food guarding. It's better to be proactive with your senior dog, making more frequent trips to the vet if necessary and having bloodwork done to test for the diseases that can commonly befall older dogs.

This is not to say that, as dogs age, they all fall apart physically and become nasty in personality. The aforementioned changes are discussed to alert owners to the things that may happen as their dogs get older. Many hardy dogs remain active and alert well into old age. However, it can be frustrating and heartbreaking for owners to see their beloved dogs change physically and temperamentally. Just know that it's the same Japanese Chin under there, and that he still loves you and appreciates your care, which he needs now more than ever.

## HOW DO I CARE FOR MY AGING DOG?

Again, every dog is an individual in terms of aging. Your dog might reach the estimated "senior" age for his breed and show no signs of

**ACCIDENT ALERT!**
Just as we puppy-proof our homes for the new member of the family, we must accident-proof our homes for the older dog. You want to create a safe environment in which the senior dog can get around easily and comfortably, with no dangers. A dog that slips and falls in old age is much more prone to injury than an adult, making accident prevention even more important. Likewise, dogs are more prone to falls in old age, as they do not have the same balance and coordination that they once had. Throw rugs on hardwood floors are slippery and pose a risk; even a throw rug on a carpeted surface could be an obstacle for the senior dog. Consider putting down non-slip surfaces or confining your dog to carpeted rooms only. Keep things consistent, as your senior dog is familiar with the layout of the home even if he cannot see as well.

tions of aging, such as graying and/or changes in sleeping, eating or toileting habits, this is a sign to set up a senior-care visit with your vet right away to make sure that these changes are not related to any health problems.

To start, senior dogs should visit the vet twice yearly for exams, routine tests and overall evaluations. Many veterinarians have special screening programs especially for senior dogs that can include a thorough physical exam; blood test to determine complete blood count; serum biochemistry test, which screens for liver, kidney and blood problems as well as cancer; urinalysis; and dental exams. With these tests, it can be determined whether your dog has any health problems; the results also establish a baseline for your pet against which future test results can be compared.

In addition to these tests, your vet may suggest additional testing, including an EKG, tests for glaucoma and other problems of the eye, chest X-rays, screening for tumors, blood pressure test, test for thyroid function and screening for parasites and reassessment of his preventive program. Your vet also will ask you questions about your dog's diet and activity level, what you feed and the amounts that you feed. This information, along with his evaluation of the dog's overall condition, will enable him to suggest proper

slowing down. However, even if he shows no outward signs of aging, he should begin a senior-care program once he reaches the determined age. He may not show it, but he's not a pup anymore! By providing him with extra attention to his veterinary care at this age, you will be practicing good preventive medicine, ensuring that the rest of your dog's life will be as long, active, happy and healthy as possible. If you do notice indica-

dietary changes, if needed.

This may seem like quite a work-up for your pet, but veterinarians advise that older dogs need more frequent attention so that any health problems can be detected as early as possible. Serious conditions like kidney disease, heart disease and cancer may not present outward symptoms, or the problem may go undetected if the symptoms are mistaken by owners as just part of the aging process.

There are some conditions more common in elderly dogs that are difficult to ignore. Cognitive dysfunction shares much in common with senility and Alzheimer's disease, and dogs are not immune. Dogs can become confused and/or disoriented, lose their house-training, have abnormal sleep-wake cycles and interact differently with their owners. Be heartened by the fact that, in some ways, there are more treatment options for dogs with cognitive dysfunction than for people with similar conditions. There is good evidence that continued stimulation in the form of games, play, training and exercise can help to maintain cognitive function. There are also medications (such as seligiline) and antioxidant-fortified senior diets that have been shown to be beneficial.

Cancer is also a condition more common in the elderly. While lung cancer, which is a major killer in humans, is relatively rare in dogs,

almost all of the cancers seen in people are also seen in pets. If pets are getting regular physical examinations, cancers are often detected early. There are a variety of cancer therapies available today, and many pets continue to live happy lives with appropriate treatment.

Degenerative joint disease, often referred to as arthritis, is another malady common to both elderly dogs and humans. A lifetime of wear and tear on joints and running around at play eventu-

### RUBDOWN REMEDY

A good remedy for an aching dog is to give him a gentle massage each day, or even a few times a day if possible. This can be especially beneficial before your dog gets out of his bed in the morning. Just as in humans, massage can decrease pain in dogs, whether the dog is arthritic or just afflicted by the stiffness that accompanies old age. Gently massage his joints and limbs, as well as petting him on his entire body. This can help his circulation and flexibility and ease any joint or muscle aches. Massaging your dog has benefits for you, too; in fact, just petting our dogs can cause reduced levels of stress and lower our blood pressure. Massage and petting also help you find any previously undetected lumps, bumps or abnormalities. Often these are not visible and only turn up by being felt.

## COPING WITH A BLIND DOG

Blindness is one of the unfortunate realities of growing old, for both dogs and humans. Owners of blind dogs should not give up hope, as most dogs adapt to their compromised state with grace and patience. A sudden loss of sight poses more stress on the dog than a gradual loss, such as that through cataracts. Some dogs may need your assistance to help them get around; others will move around seemingly uninhibited. Owners may need to retrain the dog to handle some basic tasks. Teaching commands like "Wait," "Stop" and "Slow" are handy as you help the dog learn to maneuver around his world. You are now more than the team captain, you're the coach and cheerleader! If your blind dog is showing signs of depression, it is your job to encourage him and give him moral support, just as you might for a member of your family or a good friend.

ally takes its toll and results in stiffness and difficulty in getting around. As dogs live longer and healthier lives, it is natural that they should eventually feel some of the effects of aging. Once again, if your Chin has always had regular veterinary care, he should not have been carrying extra pounds all those years and wearing those joints out before their time. If your pet was unfortunate enough to inherit hip dysplasia, osteo-chondritis dissecans or any of the other developmental orthopedic diseases, battling the onset of degenerative joint disease was probably a longstanding goal. In any case, there are now many effective remedies for managing degenerative joint disease and a number of remarkable surgeries as well.

Aside from the extra veterinary care, there is much you can do at home to keep your older dog in good condition. The dog's diet is an important factor. If your dog's appetite decreases, he will not be getting the nutrients he needs. He also will lose weight, which is unhealthy for a dog at a proper weight. Conversely, an older dog's metabolism is slower and he usually exercises less, but he should not be allowed to become obese. Obesity in an older dog is especially risky, because extra pounds mean extra stress on the body, increasing his vulnerability to heart disease. Additionally, the extra pounds make it harder for the dog to move about.

You should discuss age-related feeding changes with your vet. For a dog who has lost interest in food, it may be suggested to try some different types of food until you find something new that the dog likes. For an obese dog, a "light-"

formula dog food or reducing food portions may be advised, along with exercise appropriate to his physical condition and energy level.

As for exercise, the senior dog should not be allowed to become a "couch potato" despite his old age. He may not be able to handle the morning run, long walks and vigorous games of fetch, but he still needs to get up and get moving. Keep up with your daily walks, but keep the distances shorter and let your dog set the pace. If he gets to the point where he's not up for walks, let him stroll around the yard. On the other hand, many dogs remain very active in their senior years, so base changes to the exercise program on your own individual dog and what he's capable of. Don't worry, your Japanese Chin will let you know when it's time to rest.

Keep up with your grooming routine as you always have. Be extra-diligent about checking the skin and coat for problems. Older dogs can experience thinning coats as a normal aging process, but they can also lose hair as a result of medical problems. Some thinning is normal, but patches of baldness or the loss of significant amounts of hair is not.

Hopefully, you've been regular with brushing your dog's teeth throughout his life. Healthy teeth directly affect overall good health, and we've discussed the special importance of dental care in Toy dogs. We already know that bacteria from gum infections can enter the dog's body through the damaged gums and travel to the organs. At a stage in life when his organs don't function as well as they used to, you don't want anything to put additional strain on them. Clean teeth also contribute to a healthy immune system. Offering the dental-type chews in addition to toothbrushing can help, as they remove plaque and tartar as the dog chews.

Along with the same good care you've given him all of his life, pay a little extra attention to your dog in his senior years and keep up with twice-yearly trips to the vet. The sooner a problem is uncovered, the greater the chances of a full recovery.

### WEATHER WORRIES

Older pets are less tolerant of extremes in weather, both heat and cold. Your older dog should not spend extended periods in the sun; when outdoors in the warm weather, make sure he does not become overheated. In chilly weather, consider a sweater for your dog when outdoors and limit time spent outside. Whether or not his coat is thinning, he will need provisions to keep him warm when the weather is cold. You may even place his bed by a heating duct in your living room or bedroom.

# SHOWING YOUR

# JAPANESE CHIN

Is dog showing in your blood? Are you excited by the idea of gaiting your handsome Japanese Chin around the ring to the thunderous applause of an enthusiastic audience? Are you certain that your beloved Japanese Chin is flawless? You are not alone! Every loving owner thinks that his dog has no faults, or too few to mention. No matter how many times an owner reads the breed standard, he cannot find any faults in his aristocratic companion dog. If this sounds like you, and if you are considering entering your Japanese Chin in a dog show, here are some basic questions to ask yourself:

- Did you purchase a "show-quality" puppy from the breeder?
- Is your puppy at least six months of age?
- Does the puppy exhibit correct show type for his breed?

The Japanese Chin's elegant appearance and sparkling personality make him a dog-show favorite.

- Does your puppy have any disqualifying faults?
- Is your Japanese Chin registered with the American Kennel Club?
- How much time do you have to devote to training, grooming, conditioning and exhibiting your dog?
- Do you understand the rules and regulations of a dog show?
- Do you have time to learn how to show your dog properly?
- Do you have the financial

## AKC GROUPS

For showing purposes, the American Kennel Club divides its recognized breeds into seven groups: Toys, Sporting Dogs, Hounds, Working Dogs, Terriers, Non-Sporting Dogs and Herding Dogs. The Japanese Chin competes in the Toy Group.

conditioning and training. Very few novices, even those with good dogs, will find themselves in the winners' circle, though it does happen. Don't be disheartened, though. Every exhibitor began as a novice and worked his way up to the Group ring. It's the "working your way up" part that you must keep in mind.

Assuming that you have purchased a puppy of the correct type and quality for showing, let's begin to examine the world of showing and what's required to get started. Although the entry fee into a dog show is nominal, there are lots of other hidden costs involved with "finishing" your Japanese Chin, that is, making him a champion. Things like equipment, travel, training and conditioning all cost money. A more serious campaign will include fees for a professional handler, boarding, cross-country travel and advertising. Top-winning show dogs can represent a very considerable investment—over $100,000 has been spent in campaigning some dogs. (The investment can be less, of course, for owners who don't use professional handlers.)

Many owners, on the other hand, enter their "average" Japanese Chin in dog shows for the fun and enjoyment of it. Dog showing makes an absorbing hobby, with many rewards for dogs and owners alike. If you're having fun, meeting other people who

**If the dog is trained as a puppy to accept handling from strangers, an important part of socialization, the potential show dog will be more tolerant of the judge's evaluation when he is on the table.**

resources to invest in showing your dog?
• Will you show the dog yourself or hire a professional handler?
• Do you have a vehicle that can accommodate your weekend trips to the dog shows?

Success in the show ring requires more than a pretty face, a waggy tail and a pocketful of liver. Even though dog shows can be exciting and enjoyable, the sport of conformation makes great demands on the exhibitors and the dogs. Winning exhibitors live for their dogs, devoting time and money to their dogs' presentation,

share your interests and enjoying the overall experience, you likely will catch the "bug." Once the dog-show bug bites, its effects can last a lifetime; it's certainly much better than a deer tick! Soon you will be envisioning yourself in the center

## FOR MORE INFORMATION....

For reliable, up-to-date information about registration, dog shows and other canine competitions, contact one of the national registries by mail or via the Internet.

American Kennel Club
5580 Centerview Dr., Raleigh, NC 27606-3390
www.akc.org

United Kennel Club
100 E. Kilgore Road, Kalamazoo, MI 49002
www.ukcdogs.com

Canadian Kennel Club
89 Skyway Ave., Suite 100, Etobicoke, Ontario
M9W 6R4 Canada
www.ckc.ca

The Kennel Club
1-5 Clarges St., Piccadilly, London
W1Y 8AB, UK
www.the-kennel-club.org.uk

ring at the Westminster Kennel Club Dog Show in New York City, competing for the prestigious Best in Show cup. This magical dog show is televised annually from Madison Square Garden, and the victorious dog becomes a celebrity overnight.

## AKC CONFORMATION SHOWING

### GETTING STARTED

Visiting a dog show as a spectator is a great place to start. Pick up the show catalog to find out what time your breed is being shown, who is judging the breed and in which ring the classes will be held. To start, Japanese Chin compete against other Japanese Chin, and the winner is selected as Best of Breed by the judge. This is the procedure for each breed. At a group show, all of the Best of Breed winners go on to compete for Group One in their respective group. For example, all Best of Breed winners in a given group compete against each other; this is done for all seven groups. Finally, all seven group winners go head to head in the ring for the Best in Show award.

What most spectators don't understand is the basic idea of conformation. A dog show is often referred to as a "conformation" show. This means that the judge should decide how each dog stacks up (conforms) to the breed

Celebrating the
Chin's Japanese
origins, this
presentation in
traditional
Nipponese garb
inspired great
enthusiasm from
the spectators at
a conformation
show.

Celebrating the Chin's Japanese origins, this presentation in traditional Nipponese garb inspired great enthusiasm from the spectators at a conformation show.

standard for his given breed: how well does this Japanese Chin conform to the ideal representative detailed in the standard? Ideally, this is what happens. In reality, however, this ideal often gets

slighted as the judge compares Japanese Chin #1 to Japanese Chin #2. Again, the ideal is that each dog is judged based on his merits in comparison to his breed standard, not in comparison to the other dogs in the ring. It is easier for judges to compare dogs of the same breed to decide which they think is the better specimen; in the Group and Best in Show ring, however, it is very difficult to compare one breed to another, like apples to oranges. Thus the dog's conformation to the breed standard—not to mention advertising dollars and good handling—is essential to success in conformation shows. The dog described in the standard (the standard for each AKC breed is written and approved by the breed's national parent club and then submitted to the AKC for approval) is the perfect dog of that breed, and breeders keep their eye on the standard when they choose which dogs to breed, hoping to get closer and closer to the ideal with each litter.

Another good first step for the novice is to join a dog club. You will be astonished by the many and different kinds of dog clubs in the country, with about 5,000 clubs holding events every year. Most clubs require that prospective new members present two letters of recommendation from existing members. Perhaps you've made some friends visiting a show held by a particular club and you would like to join that club. Dog clubs may specialize in a single breed, like a local or regional Japanese Chin club, or in a specific pursuit, such as obedience, tracking or hunting tests. There are all-breed

> **MEET THE AKC**
> The American Kennel Club is the main governing body of the dog sport in the United States. Founded in 1884, the AKC consists of 500 or more independent dog clubs plus 4,500 affiliated clubs, all of which follow the AKC rules and regulations. Additionally, the AKC maintains a registry for pure-bred dogs in the US and works to preserve the integrity of the sport and its continuation in the country. Over 1,000,000 dogs are registered each year, representing over 150 recognized breeds. There are over 15,000 competitive events held annually for which over 2,000,000 dogs enter to participate. Dogs compete to earn over 40 different titles, from champion to Companion Dog to Master Agility Champion.

clubs for all dog enthusiasts; they sponsor special training days, seminars on topics like grooming or handling or lectures on breeding or canine genetics. There are also clubs that specialize in certain types of dogs, like herding dogs, hunting dogs, companion dogs, etc.

A parent club is the national organization, sanctioned by the AKC, which promotes and safeguards its breed in the country. The Japanese Chin Club of America (JCCA) was formed in 1912 and can be contacted on the Internet at www.chinamerica.org.

The parent club holds specialty shows each year, usually in different regions of the country, in which many of the country's top dogs, handlers and breeders gather to compete. At a specialty show, only members of a single breed are invited to participate. JCCA specialties offer competition, education, socializing and fun for Chin and fanciers from across the country. For more information about dog clubs in your area, contact the AKC at www.akc.org on the Internet or write them at their Raleigh, NC address.

### How Shows Are Organized

Three kinds of conformation shows are offered by the AKC. There is the all-breed show, in which all AKC-recognized breeds can compete; the specialty show, which is for one breed only and usually sponsored by the breed's parent club and the group show, for all breeds in one of the AKC's seven groups. The Japanese Chin competes in the Toy Group.

For a dog to become an AKC champion of record, the dog must earn 15 points at shows. The points must be awarded by at least three different judges and must include two "majors" under different judges. A "major" is a three-, four- or five-point win, and the number of points per win is determined by the number of dogs competing in the show on that day. (Dogs that are absent or are

| **EXPRESS YOURSELF**
The most intangible of all canine attributes, expression speaks to the character of the breed, attained by the combined features of the head. The shape and balance of the dog's skull, the color and position of the eyes and the size and carriage of the head mingle to produce the correct expression of the breed. A judge may approach a dog and determine instantly whether the dog's face portrays the desired impression for the breed, conveying nobility, intelligence and alertness among other specifics of the breed standard.

excused are not counted.) The number of points that are awarded varies from breed to breed. More dogs are needed to attain a major in more popular breeds, and fewer dogs are needed in less popular breeds. Yearly, the AKC evaluates the number of dogs in competition in each division (there are 14 divisions in all, based on geography) and may or may not change the numbers of dogs required for each number of points. For example, a major in Division 2 (Delaware, New Jersey and Pennsylvania) recently required 17 dogs or 16 bitches for a three-point major, 29 dogs or 27 bitches for a four-point major and 51 dogs or 46 bitches for a five-point major. The Japanese Chin attracts numerically proportionate representation at all-breed shows.

Only one dog and one bitch of each breed can win points at a given show. There are no "co-ed" classes except for champions of record. Dogs and bitches do not compete against each other until they are champions. Dogs that are not champions (referred to as "class dogs") compete in one of five classes. The class in which a dog is entered depends on age and previous show wins. First there is the Puppy Class (sometimes divided further into classes for 6- to 9-month-olds and 9- to 12-month-olds); next is the Novice Class (for dogs that have no points toward their championship and whose only first-place wins have come in the Puppy Class or the Novice Class, the latter class limited to three first places); then there is the American-bred Class (for dogs bred in the US); the Bred-by-Exhibitor Class (for dogs handled by their breeders or by immediate family members of their breeders) and the Open Class (for any non-champions). Any dog may enter the Open Class, regardless of age or win history, but, to be competitive, the dog should be older and have ring experience.

The judge at the show begins judging the male dogs in the Puppy Class(es) and proceeds through the other classes. The judge awards first through fourth place in each class. The first-place winners of each class then compete with one another in the Winners Class to determine Winners Dog. The judge then starts over with the bitches, beginning with the Puppy Class(es) and proceeding up to the Winners Class to award Winners Bitch, just as he did with the dogs. A Reserve Winners Dog and Reserve Winners Bitch are also selected; they could

## CANINE GOOD CITIZEN® PROGRAM

Have you ever considered getting your dog "certified"? The AKC's Canine Good Citizen® Program affords your dog just that opportunity. Your dog shows that he is a well-behaved canine citizen, using the basic training and good manners you have taught him, by taking a series of ten tests that illustrate that he can behave properly at home, in a public place and around other dogs. The tests are administered by participating dog clubs, colleges, 4-H clubs, Scouts and other community groups and are open to all pure-bred and mixed-breed dogs. Upon passing the ten tests, the suffix CGC is then applied to your dog's name.

The ten tests are: 1. Accepting a friendly stranger; 2. Sitting politely for petting; 3. Appearance and grooming; 4. Walking on a lead; 5. Walking through a group of people; 6. Sit, down and stay on command; 7. Coming when called; 8. Meeting another dog; 9. Calm reaction to distractions; 10. Separation from owner.

be awarded the points in the case of a disqualification.

The Winners Dog and Winners Bitch are the two that are awarded the points for their breed. They then go on to compete with any champions of record (often called "specials") of their breed that are entered in the show. The champions may be dogs or bitches; in this class, all are shown together. The judge reviews the Winners Dog and Winners Bitch along with all of the champions to select the Best of Breed winner. The Best of Winners is selected between the Winners Dog and Winners Bitch; if one of these two is selected Best of Breed as well, he or she is automatically determined Best of Winners. Lastly, the judge selects Best of Opposite Sex to the Best of Breed winner. The Best of Breed winner then goes on to the group competition.

At a group or all-breed show, the Best of Breed winners from each breed are divided into their respective groups to compete against one another for Group One through Group Four. Group One (first place) is awarded to the dog that best lives up to the ideal for his breed as described in the standard. A group judge, therefore, must have a thorough working knowledge of many breed standards. After placements have been made in each group, the seven Group One winners (from the Toy Group, Sporting Group,

Hound Group, etc.) compete against each other for the top honor, Best in Show.

**ENTERING SHOWS**

There are different ways to find out about dog shows in your area. The American Kennel Club's monthly magazine, the *American Kennel Gazette* is accompanied by the *Events Calendar*; this magazine is available through subscription. You can also look on the AKC's and your parent club's websites for information and check the event listings in your local newspaper.

Your Chin must be six months of age or older and registered with the AKC in order to be entered in AKC-sanctioned shows in which there are classes for the Japanese Chin. Your Japanese Chin also must not possess any disqualifying faults and must be sexually intact. The reason for the latter is simple: dog shows are the proving grounds to determine which dogs and bitches are worthy of being bred. If they cannot be bred, that defeats the purpose! On that note, only dogs that have achieved championships, thus proving their excellent quality, should be bred. If you have spayed or neutered your dog, however, there are many AKC and breed club events other than conformation, such as obedience, agility, tracking, rally and the Canine Good Citizen® program, in which you and your Chin can participate.

You chose your dog because something clicked the minute you set eyes on him. Or perhaps it seemed that the dog selected you and that's what clinched the deal. Either way, you are now investing time and money in this dog, a true pal and an outstanding member of the family. Everything about him is perfect...well, almost perfect. Remember, he is a dog! For that matter, how does he think *you're* doing?

## UNDERSTANDING THE CANINE MINDSET

For starters, you and your dog are on different wavelengths. Your dog is similar to a toddler in that both live in the present tense only. A dog's view of life is based primarily on cause and effect, which is similar to the old saying, "Nothing teaches a youngster to hang on like falling off the swing." If your dog stumbles down a flight of three steps, hopefully that will teach him to walk more carefully next time—or he may avoid the stairs altogether.

Your dog makes connections based on the fact that he lives in the present, so when he is doing something and you interrupt to dispense praise or a correction, a connection, positive or negative, is made. To the dog, that's like one plus one equals two! In the same sense, it's also easy to see that when your timing is off, you will cause an incorrect connection. The one-plus-one way of thinking is why you must never scold a dog for behavior that took place an hour, 15 minutes or even 5 seconds ago. But it is also why, when your timing is perfect, you can teach him to do all kinds of wonderful things—as soon as he has made that essential connection. What helps the process is his desire to please you and to have

### DOMINANCE

Dogs are born with dominance skills, meaning that they can be quite clever in trying to get their way. The "Follow-me" trot to the cookie jar is an example. The toy dropped in your lap says "Play with me." The leash delivered to you along with an excited look means "Take me for a walk." These are all good-natured dominant behaviors. Ask your dog to sit before agreeing to his request and you'll remain "top dog."

your approval.

There are behaviors we admire in dogs, such as friendliness and obedience, as well as those behaviors that cause problems to a varying degree. The dog owner who encounters minor behavioral problems is wise to solve them promptly or get professional help. Bad behaviors are not corrected by repeatedly shouting "No" or getting angry with the dog. Only the giving of praise and approval for good behavior lets your dog understand right from wrong. The longer a bad behavior is allowed to continue, the harder it is to overcome. A responsible breeder is often able to help. Each dog is unique, so try not to compare your dog's behavior with your neighbor's dog or the one you had as a child.

Have your veterinarian check the dog to see whether a behavior problem could have a physical cause. An earache or toothache, for example, could be the reason for a dog to snap at you if you were to touch his head when putting on his leash. A sharp correction from you would only increase the behavior. When a physical basis is eliminated, and if the problem is not something you understand or can cope with, ask for the name of a behavioral specialist, preferably one who is familiar with the Japanese Chin. Be sure to keep the breeder informed of your progress.

Many things, such as environ-ment and inherited traits, form the basic behavior of a dog, just as in humans. You also must factor into his temperament the purpose for which your dog was originally bred. The major obstacle lies in the dog's inability to explain his behavior to us in a way that we understand. The one thing you should not do is to give up and abandon your dog. Somewhere a misunderstanding has occurred, but, with help and patient understanding on your part, you should be able to work out the majority of bothersome behaviors.

**SEPARATION ANXIETY**
Any behaviorist will tell you that separation anxiety is the most common problem about which pet owners complain. Separation anxiety is a real problem in dogs and one that should not be dismissed as "canine

---

**ONE BITE TOO MANY**
It's natural for puppies to bite in play, but you must teach your puppy that this is unacceptable in human circles. Relax your hand, say "No bite" and offer him a toy. An adolescent dog is testing his dominance and will bite as a way of disobeying you. If not stopped in puppyhood, you will end up with an adult dog that will bite aggressively. All adult biting should be considered serious and dealt with by a professional.

psychobabble." It is, however, also one of the easiest to prevent. Unfortunately, a behaviorist usually is not consulted until the dog is a stressed-out, neurotic mess. At that stage, it is indeed a problem that requires the help of a professional.

Training the puppy to the fact that people in the house come and go is essential in order to avoid this anxiety. Leaving the puppy in his crate or a confined area while family members go in and out, and stay out for longer and longer periods of time, is the basic way to desensitize the pup to the family's frequent departures. If you are at home most of every day, make it a point to go out for at least an hour or two whenever possible.

How you leave is vital to the dog's reaction. Your dog is no fool. He knows the difference between sweats and business suits, jeans and dresses. He sees you pat your pocket to check for your wallet, open your briefcase, check that you have your cell phone or pick up the car keys. He knows from the hurry of the kids in the morning that they're off to school until afternoon. Lipstick? Aftershave lotion? Lunch boxes? Every move you make registers in his sensory perception and memory. Your puppy knows more about your departures than the FBI. You can't get away with a thing!

Before you got dressed, you

---

**"LEAVE IT"**

Watch your puppy like a hawk to be certain it's a toy he's chewing, not your wallet. When you catch him in the act, tell him "Leave it!" and substitute a proper toy. Chewing on anything other than his own safe toys is countered by spraying the desirable (to the dog) object with a foul-tasting product (safe for dogs and made to deter chewing) and being more diligent in your observations of his chewing habits. When you can't supervise, it's crate time for Fido. Although all puppies chew, Chin owners are fortunate that their pups grow out of this habit, as adult Chin are not typically chewers.

---

checked the dog's water bowl and his supply of toys (including a long-lasting chew toy), and turned the radio on low. You will leave him in what he considers his "safe" area, not with total freedom of the house. If you've invested in child safety gates, you can be reasonably sure that he'll remain in the designated area. Don't give him access to a window where he can watch you leave the house. If you're leaving for an hour or two, just put him into his crate with a safe toy.

Now comes the test! You are ready to walk out the door. Do not give your Chin a big hug and a fond farewell. Do not drag out a long goodbye. Those are the very things that jump-start separation anxiety. Toss a biscuit into the dog's area, call out "So long, pooch" and close the door. You're gone. The chances are that the dog may bark a couple of times, or maybe whine once or twice, and then settle down to enjoy his biscuit and take a lovely nap, especially if you took him for a nice long walk after breakfast. As he grows up, the barks and whines will stop because it's an old routine, so why should he make the effort?

When you first brought home the puppy, the come-and-go routine was intermittent and constant. He was put into his crate

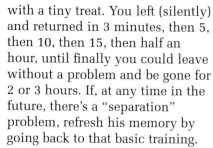

with a tiny treat. You left (silently) and returned in 3 minutes, then 5, then 10, then 15, then half an hour, until finally you could leave without a problem and be gone for 2 or 3 hours. If, at any time in the future, there's a "separation" problem, refresh his memory by going back to that basic training.

Now comes the next most important part—your return. Do not make a big production of coming home. "Hi, poochie" is as grand a greeting as he needs. When you've taken off your hat and coat, tossed your briefcase on the hall table and glanced at the mail, and the dog has settled down from the excitement of seeing you "in person" from his confined area, then go and give him a warm, friendly greeting. A potty trip is needed and a walk would be appreciated, since he's been such a good dog.

**MATTERS OF SEX**
For whatever reasons, real or imagined, most people tend to have a preference in choosing between a male and female puppy. Some, but not all, of the undesirable traits attributed to the sex of the dog can be suppressed by early spaying or neutering. The major advantage, of course, is that a neutered male or a spayed female will not be adding to the overpopulation of dogs.

An unaltered male will mark territory by lifting his leg

---

### DIGGING OUT

Some dogs love to dig. Others wouldn't think of it. Digging is considered "self-rewarding behavior" because it's fun! Of all the digging solutions offered by the experts, most are only marginally successful and none is guaranteed to work. The best cure is prevention, which means removing the dog from the offending site when he digs as well as distracting him when you catch him digging so that he turns his attentions elsewhere. That means that you have to supervise your dog's yard time. An unsupervised digger can create havoc with your landscaping or, worse, run away!

**BARKING**

Barking is a dog's way of "talking," and it can be rightly and thankfully said that the Chin is the most reticent of the Toy breeds. This is the least yappy of the lap dogs! While not as vocal as most other Toy dogs, they tend to use their purposeful barks as alarm dogs for their families. This type of barking should *not* be discouraged. If an intruder came into your home in the middle of the night and your Chin barked a warning, you would properly deem your dog a hero, a wonderful watchdog for your home.

Excessive habitual barking in the Chin is very rare, but if it should occur it must be corrected early on. If you give him a command such as "Quiet" and praise him after he has stopped barking for a few seconds, he will get the idea that being "quiet" is what you want him to do.

everywhere, leaving a few drops of urine indoors on your furniture and appliances, and outside on everything he passes. It is difficult to catch him in the act, because he leaves only a few drops each time, but it is very hard to eliminate the odor. Thus the cycle begins, because the odor will entice him to mark that spot again.

If you have bought a bitch with the intention of breeding her, be sure you know what you are getting into. She will go through one or two periods of estrus each year. Generally, a bitch's cycles last about three weeks each, but Chin females tend to experience longer heat cycles. During those times, she will have to be kept confined to protect your furniture and to protect her from being bred by a male other than the one you have selected. Breeding should never be undertaken to "show the kids the miracle of birth." Bitches can die giving birth, and the

puppies may also die. The dam often exhibits what is called "maternal aggression" after the pups are born. Her intention is to protect her pups, but in fact she can be extremely vicious. Breeding should be left to the experienced breeders, who do so for the betterment of the breed and with much research and planning behind each mating.

Mounting is not unusual in dogs, male or female. Puppies do it to each other and adults do it regardless of sex, because it is not so much a sexual act as it is one of dominance. It becomes very annoying when the dog mounts your legs, the kids or the couch cushions; in these and any other instances of mounting, he should be corrected. Touching sometimes stimulates the dog, so pulling the dog off by his collar or leash, together with a consistent and stern "Off!" command, usually eliminates the behavior.

Chin would much rather eat your table food than the balanced diet you've selected for them. Never offer your food scraps from the table, or you will have to contend with a beggar at every meal in your own kitchen.

### FOOD-RELATED PROBLEMS

Face it. All dogs are beggars. Food is the motivation for everything we want our dogs to do and, when you combine that with their innate ability to "con" us in order to get their way, it's a wonder there aren't far more obese dogs in the world.

Who can resist the bleeding-heart look that says "I'm starving," or the paw that gently pats your knee and gives you a knowing look, or the whining "please" or even the total body language of a perfect sit beneath the cookie jar. No one who professes to love his dog can turn down the pleas of his clever canine's performances every time. One thing is for sure, though: definitely do not allow begging at the table. Family meals do not include your dog.

Control your dog's begging habit by making your dog work for his rewards. Ignore his begging when you can. Utilize the obedience commands you've taught your dog. Use "Off" for the pawing. A sit or even a long down will interrupt the whining. His reward in these situations is definitely not a treat! Casual verbal praise is enough. Be sure all members of the family follow the same rules. There is a different type of begging that does demand your immediate response and that is the appeal to be let (or taken) outside! Usually that is a quick paw or small whine to get your attention, followed by a race to the door. This type of begging needs your quick attention and approval. Of course, a really smart dog will soon figure out how to cut you off at the pass and direct you to that cookie jar on your way to the door! Some dogs are always one step ahead of us.

Stealing food is a problem only if you are not paying attention. A dog can't steal food that is not within his reach. Leaving your dog in the kitchen with the roast beef on the table is asking for trouble. Putting cheese and crackers on the coffee table also requires a watchful eye to stop the thief in his tracks. The word to use (one word, remember, even if it's two words pronounced as one) is "Leave it!" Instead of preceding it with yet another "No," try using a guttural sound like "Aagh!" That sounds more like a warning growl to the dog and therefore has instant meaning.

Canine thieves are in their element when little kids are carrying cookies in their hands! Your dog will think he's been exceptionally clever if he causes a child to drop a cookie. Bonanza! The easiest solution is to keep dog and children separated at snack time. You must also be sure that the children understand that they must not tease the dog with food—his or theirs. Your dog does not mean to bite the kids, but when he snatches at a tidbit so near the level of his mouth, it can result in an unintended nip.

## EATING EXCREMENT

The unpleasant subject of dogs' eating their own feces, known as coprophagia, can be dealt with relatively easily even though no one is exactly sure why dogs do this. Some say it is primordial,

while others feel that it indicates a lack of something in the diet (but there's no agreement as to what that "something" is). Unless the dog has worms, feces eating cannot make him sick, but that is no reason to allow it to continue. There are products said to alleviate the problem, but check with your vet before adding anything to your puppy's diet. Sprinkling hot pepper on the feces is an after-the-fact solution. Prevention is the better way to go.

When you house-trained your dog, you took him outside on a leash and stayed with him until he did his business. Afterward, you cleaned up the feces. You were not giving him any opportunity to indulge in this strange canine habit. Now that your dog goes outside alone, watch to see that it doesn't start. At his first sign of interest in his own excrement, or that of any other animal, give him a sharp "No! Leave it!" and then bring the dog indoors so you can do your clean-up job. To clean up after your dog on the street, use a plastic bag over your hand to pick up the feces. In your yard, a "poop-scoop" is the easiest answer.

Cat feces entice many dogs, too. If you have cats, look into the litter boxes that are made with narrow tunnel entrances to deter all but the most insistent of dogs. Keep the litter clean and the box in a spot that's inaccessible to your dog.

### FOUR ON THE FLOOR

You must discourage your dog from jumping up to get attention or for any other reason. To do so, turn away from the dog when he is attempting to jump up on you. "Four on the floor" requires praise. Once the dog sits on command, prevent him from attempting to jump again by asking him to sit-stay before petting him. Back away if he breaks the sit.

# INDEX

# My Japanese Chin

PUT YOUR PUPPY'S FIRST PICTURE HERE

Dog's Name _____

Date _____ Photographer _____